Secondary Science

PLACE IN RETURN BOX to remove this checkout from your record.
TO AVOID FINES return on or before date due.
MAY BE RECALLED with earlier due date if requested.

DATE DUE	DATE DUE	DATE DUE

5/08 K:/Proj/Acc&Pres/CIRC/DateDue.indd

Education at SAGE

SAGE is a leading international publisher of journals, books, and electronic media for academic, educational, and professional markets.

Our education publishing includes:

- accessible and comprehensive texts for aspiring education professionals and practitioners looking to further their careers through continuing professional development

- inspirational advice and guidance for the classroom

- authoritative state of the art reference from the leading authors in the field

Find out more at: **www.sagepub.co.uk/education**

Secondary Science 11 to 16

A Practical Guide

Gren Ireson, Mark Crowley, Ruth Richards
and John Twidle

Los Angeles | London | New Delhi
Singapore | Washington DC

SAGE Publications Ltd
1 Oliver's Yard
55 City Road
London EC1Y 1SP

SAGE Publications Inc.
2455 Teller Road
Thousand Oaks, California 91320

SAGE Publications India Pvt Ltd
B 1/I 1 Mohan Cooperative Industrial Area
Mathura Road
New Delhi 110 044

SAGE Publications Asia-Pacific Pte Ltd
33 Pekin Street #02-01
Far East Square
Singapore 048763

Library of Congress Control Number: 2009934562

British Library Cataloguing in Publication data

A catalogue record for this book is available from the British Library

ISBN 978-1-84920-125-4
ISBN 978-1-84920-126-1 (pbk)

Typeset by C&M Digitals, Pvt Ltd, Chennai, India
Printed in Great Britain by CPI Antony Rowe, Chippenham, Wiltshire
Printed on paper from sustainable resources

Mixed Sources
Product group from well-managed
forests and other controlled sources
www.fsc.org Cert no. SGS-COC-002953
© 1996 Forest Stewardship Council
FSC

Contents

About the authors

Editor

Gren Ireson is Professor of Science Education at Nottingham Trent University. Gren was previously Senior Lecturer at Loughborough University where he returned to higher education following several years teaching in UK secondary schools.

Contributors

Mark Crowley is a Teaching Research Fellow in the Centre for Effective Learning in Science, Nottingham Trent University.

Ruth Richards is Senior Lecturer in Science Education and subject leader for the PGCE and Subject Knowledge Enhancement courses in science at Nottingham Trent University. Ruth is also an examiner for A-level geology.

John Twidle is Lecturer in Science Education and subject leader for the PGCE and MSc in Science Education programmes at Loughborough University.

Acknowledgements

First we would like to acknowledge the contribution of all the trainee and practising teachers we have worked with for raising the questions we have attempted to address. In our view Science is more about the ability to ask the right questions, rather than knowing all the answers.

Secondly we would like to thank Lesley, Esmé, Jacob, Graeme, Linda, Victoria, Clare, Natasha and Jim for their encouragement, support and giving us time to write.

Finally our thanks must go to Sage Publications for steering this work from proposal to publication.

Introduction

Our approach to the learning and teaching of science is based loosely on a constructivist approach which both challenges and engages the learner. While we see science as being very much a *hands-on* activity we like to take this a stage further and make science a *minds-on* activity.

For teachers, our experience has shown that those new to teaching or those teaching outside their specialism have three key questions:

- Do I have the subject knowledge?
- How does the subject link to the National Curriculum?
- How can I make the topic engaging, fun and *minds on*?

This book, over twelve chapters, addresses these questions by:

- linking to the English, Irish, Scottish and Welsh curricula;
- linking to 'How Science Works';
- setting the scene with Key Stage 3 subject knowledge;
- developing Key Stage 4 subject knowledge;
- presenting fun, *minds-on* activities; and
- providing references and further reading.

The twelve chapters are structured around four sections which draw together key areas of science, biology, chemistry, physics and earth science, and it is hoped that this will make navigation easier for the reader.

Each chapter takes a standard approach, starting with questions to test your knowledge (the answers are addressed during the main text), explanatory text and practical work, and further reading. Where appropriate, *practical activities* and *engaging activities* are also suggested.

The authors recognize that this book is not a replacement for the vast number of texts available but, by drawing on their collective experience of both school and higher education, this book addresses areas that trainee and practising teachers have found difficult in the past. Having worked through this book and having involved yourself in the practical activities, it is expected that you will have developed sufficient confidence and competence to tackle areas not explored here.

Section 1

Beginnings and development of living things

This section has a biological focus which should help to develop your understanding of a number of biological processes. In this section, of two chapters, you will be introduced to the science of:

- cells – the building blocks of living organisms;
- reproduction – the continuation of life; and
- genetics – the variation and inheritance of characteristics.

This links to, and will help you deliver, the various national curricula for England, Ireland, Scotland and Wales as set out below.

By working through this section it is expected that you will be able to describe and explain:

- the various functions of animal and plant cells;
- the process of reproduction;
- the process of genetic inheritance; and
- the passing on of characteristics.

Please turn over to see how this section relates to your curriculum.

National Curriculum for England	Junior Certificate Science Syllabus	Environmental Studies – Society, Science and Technology	Science in the National Curriculum for Wales
KS3, 3.3	**1B4** Reproductive system:	Living things and the processes of life:	**KS3, 1** Life Processes and Cell Activity:
a life processes are supported by the organisation of cells into tissues, organs and body systems	male and female reproductive systems menstrual cycle fertilization and pregnancy contraception	Variety and characteristic features	**1** That animals and plants are made up of cells
b the human reproductive cycle includes adolescence, fertilisation and foetal development		Developing an understanding of the characteristic features of the main groups of plants and animals, including humans and microorganisms	**2** The functions of the cell membrane, cytoplasm and nucleus in plant and animal cells
c conception, growth, development, behaviour and health can be affected by diet, drugs and disease	**1B5** Genetics: inheritable and non-inheritable characteristics chromosomes and genes		**3** The functions of chloroplasts and cell walls in plant cells
d all living things show variation, can be classified and are interdependent, interacting with each other and their environment		The principles of genetics are also considered	**4** Variation, Classification and Inheritance
e behaviour is influenced by internal and external factors and can be investigated and measured	**1C1** Living things: life processes and common characteristics of living organisms relationship between cells, tissues, organs and systems	The processes of life	**KS4, 1** Life Processes and Cell Activity:
		Developing an understanding of growth and development and life cycles, including cells and cell processes	**1** That cells have a nucleus, a cell membrane and cytoplasm
KS4, 5		The main organs of the human body and their functions are also considered	**2** That the nucleus contains chromosomes that carry the genes
b variation within species can lead to evolutionary changes and similarities and differences between species can be measured and classified			**3** Variation, Inheritance and Evolution:
c the ways in which organisms function are related to the genes in their cells			**1** That sexual reproduction is a source of genetic variation, while asexual reproduction produces clones
			2 That mutation, which may be beneficial or harmful, is a source of genetic variation and has a number of causes
			3 How gender is determined in humans
			4 The mechanism of monohybrid inheritance where there are dominant and recessive alleles
			5 That some diseases are inherited
			6 The basic principles of cloning, selective breeding and genetic engineering
			7 The potential benefits and ethical dilemmas posed by advances in cloning and genetic engineering

1 Looking at life
Ruth Richards

This chapter covers:

- the characteristics of life
- cell structure
- practical techniques for making slides
- levels of organization
- diffusion and osmosis.

 Test your own knowledge

Before reading the material in this chapter test your current knowledge with the following questions:

1. How do we know something is alive?
2. What is a cell? What are the main components of an animal and a plant cell? Which components are shared by both plant and animal cells?
3. What is the function of each cell component?
4. How do substances get in and out of cells? Are there any rules for this?
5. What is the definition of a cell, an organelle, a tissue and an organism?

What is life?

Everything that is considered to be alive carries out the seven characteristics of life. These are known by the mnemonic MRS GREN (Movement, Respiration, Sensitivity, Growth, Reproduction, Excretion and Nutrition).

The following information can be used to construct a card sort for students to recap this topic from Key Stage 3:

- **Movement:** Organisms may move all or parts of their bodies towards or away from influences that are important to them. For example, a plant may move its leaves towards the sun.
- **Respiration:** The release of energy stored in food, such as glucose, to provide power for the cell to function. The energy currency of the cell is adenosine tri-phosphate, or ATP for short. Respiration takes place in the mitochondria of every cell.
- **Sensitivity:** Awareness of the organisms' surroundings. This may be complex, such as the passage of nerve impulses, or simpler, such as the growth of plant roots down into the soil.
- **Growth:** An increase in size, such as the division of one cell into two identical cells (mitosis).
- **Reproduction:** The formation of more individuals from one parent (asexually) or two parents (sexually).
- **Excretion:** Getting rid of the products of the chemical reactions that have taken place in the organism (metabolism). Metabolism occurs at a cellular level, and so excretion includes getting rid of water and carbon dioxide. (Not getting rid of solid waste!)
- **Nutrition:** Using a food source to release energy for cell function. This is either autotrophic, when plants make their own food by photosynthesis and then metabolise it, or heterotrophic, when ready-made food is taken into an organism.

The cell

What is a cell? A cell is a single unit that can function on its own and can divide to form other cells of the same type. It is a package that contains all the 'bits' needed to be alive. These component parts of cells are called organelles. The cell itself is the basic unit of life, and all multicellular organisms are derived originally from one cell. It should be noted that animal cells are generally smaller than plant cells and lack some of the cell contents of plant cells.

How science works

The cell was first discovered by Robert Hooke in 1665. He used a basic microscope to look at thin slices of cork (from a cork tree) and he saw boxes that reminded him of monks' rooms or cells. Hence the name – 'cell'.

A good way to get students to compare animal and plant cells is by using a Venn diagram. This helps assess prior learning and gives you the basis to discuss any misconceptions that the students may have.

Provide the students with a list of the cell components and ask them to categorize these as being present in animals only, plants only or in both animal and plant cells (a shared field in the centre). Students could be asked to extend this by underlining the components that cannot be seen by using an ordinary light microscope, such as the ones they may use in class.

The completed example is shown in Figure 1.1. The words underlined are those components that cannot be seen through a standard light microscope as used in schools.

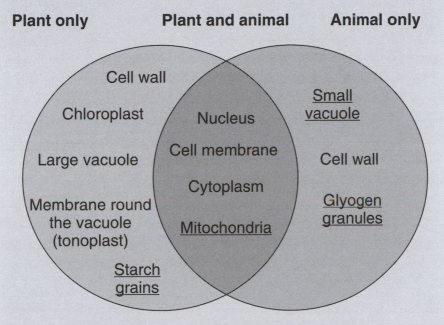

Figure 1.1   Venn diagram comparing plant and animal cells

The cell: card sort

The list of cell components, their description and function can be organized as a card sort. This can be seen in the card sort exercise shown in Figure 1.2, which can be easily differentiated by the removal of the more complex components. Simply cut these out in advance of the lesson.

(Continued)

(Continued)

Cell component	Description	Function
Nucleus	Largest cell organelle. Contains strands of DNA. Appears patchy and dark coloured when a stain is added.	Regulates cell activities. Stores information which it passes on by cell division (mitosis and meiosis).
Cell membrane	Exterior layer of the cell. Composed of protein and oil (lipid).	Keeps all cell contents together. Is selectively permeable as it regulates what enters and leaves the cell.
Cell wall	Made of strong cellulose. Permeable to water and other substances.	Gives shape and support to the plant cell. Resists water movement into the cell when the cell is turgid.
Cytoplasm	Jelly-like substance (consistency of raw egg white). Composed mainly of water.	Supports the organelles. Store of water and/or pigments.
Chloroplast	Large green-coloured organelles.	To carry out photosynthesis. This uses trapped light energy to combine carbon dioxide and water to form glucose and oxygen. The glucose stores energy in its bonds.
Vacuoles	Large permanent vacuoles are found in the centre of plant cells. Small non-permanent vacuoles are found scattered throughout the cytoplasm in animal cells.	Storage of materials such as food or pigments and water control. Transport of substances around the cell and secretion of substances outside the cell (e.g. mucus or hormones).
Starch grain	Grains found inside plant cells. Small glucose molecules are converted into starch so that they can be stored.	Storage of food until needed. Glucose cannot be stored as it moves by diffusion and is therefore not kept in one place.
Glycogen granules and fat droplets	Granules or droplets found within the cytoplasm of animal cells.	Storage of food until needed.
Mitochondria	Organelles (about 5 nm) found in the cytoplasm.	Carries out aerobic respiration in cells.
Ribosomes	Tiny organelles (20 nm) found in the cytoplasm.	Make proteins by assembling amino acids in chains.

Figure 1.2 Card sort activity: the cell

Common misconceptions include students using the terms 'cell wall' and 'cell membrane' interchangeably and thinking that mitochondria can be seen with a light microscope. It should be noted that the cell membrane and tonoplast are difficult to see in many plant cells. The position of these can be highlighted during a practical by using the purple epidermis layers between the fleshy leaves in red onions. The position of the cytoplasm can be located because the cell contents are suspended within it.

Levels of organization: card sort

Cells can be added together to make increasingly complex organisms and parts of organisms. This can be seen in the card sort exercise in Figure 1.3.

Level of organization	Description	Example
Atom	Fundamental unit of matter	Hydrogen 
Molecule	At least two atoms held together by chemical bonds	Water 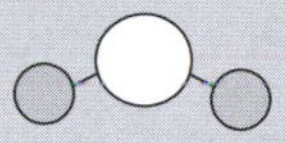
Organelle	Small units in cells that do one particular job	Mitochondrion 
Cell	The basic unit of life that can function independently	Sperm cell 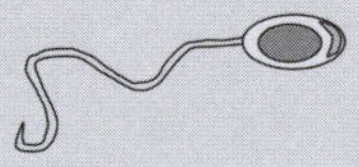
Tissue	Collection of similar cells that perform the same job	Muscle 
Organ	Collection of tissues that perform a specific or several functions	Liver 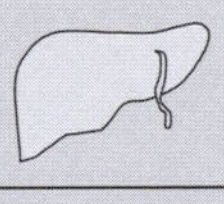
Organ system	Collection of organs that work together to carry out a specific task	Digestive system 
Organism	A group of organ systems making up an individual	Mouse 

Figure 1.3   Card sort activity: levels of organization

Practical activity

Looking at animal cells

You can look at your own cells, but this requires you to take a sample of your own cheek cells (epithelial cells). The students quite like this as they are looking at their own cells – a rare opportunity.

Health and safety

You must check the health and safety regulations where you teach as rules vary from school to school and from county to county. Your senior technician or health and safety officer will be able to say if any practical is banned in your school. Alternatives are usually available if this is the case.

If you can go ahead and do this practical, you must make sure you use a clean scraper or cotton bud and dispose of it in accordance with the regulations in your school. Ideally the scrapers should have been dry sterilized before use and be disposed of in disinfectant afterwards.

Be careful not to focus direct sunlight through the microscope because this can damage your eyes.

Method

The method is as follows (see also Figure 1.4). Take a clean scraper and rub it on the inside of your cheek. Around ten scrapes are enough to get a decent

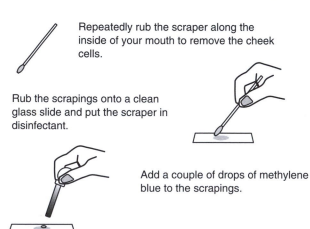

Repeatedly rub the scraper along the inside of your mouth to remove the cheek cells.

Rub the scrapings onto a clean glass slide and put the scraper in disinfectant.

Add a couple of drops of methylene blue to the scrapings.

Cover the scrapings with a cover slip by lowering it slowly down using a dissection needle.

Figure 1.4   Preparing an animal cell slide

sample, but be careful to collect cheek cells and not saliva. Rub the scrapings on to a clean glass slide and put the scraper in disinfectant. Add a couple of drops of methylene blue, being careful not to stain your hands or clothes. Cover the scrapings with a cover slip by lowering it slowly down using a dissection needle. The stain will spread out under the cover slip. Examine using a microscope, low power first, and then switch to a higher magnification. The students should be able to see cell membranes, nuclei and the cytoplasm. They should recognize that the cells are broadly square shaped, because they would fit rather like paving flags forming the epithelial layer inside your cheek.

Practical activity

Looking at plant cells

You can look at the cells of the onion to see typical plant cells. The best results are found when you use red onions. You will be using the thin epidermis layers between the fleshy leaves as these are only a few cells thick.

Health and safety

Care should be taken if the students are using scalpals, and the appropriate warnings should be given prior to their use. Goggles should be worn when using the iodine solution and care should be taken to avoid contact with the skin. Be careful not to focus direct sunlight through the microscope because this can damage your eyes.

Method

The method is as follows (see also Figure 1.5). Take the epidermis layer from between the fleshy part of the onion. The darker-coloured cells are best as they contain the pigments in the cytoplasm and the vacuoles. Cut a piece approximately 1 cm², using a scalpel. Place this on to a slide and ensure that it is lying flat. It is easiest to do this using a pair of tweezers. Add one or two drops of dilute iodine solution, being careful not to stain your hands or clothes. Cover the epidermis layer with a cover slip by lowering it slowly down using a dissection needle. The stain will spread out under the cover slip. Examine using a microscope, low power first, and then switch to a higher magnification. You will be able to see elongate cells with distinct nuclei and the clear double cell walls of two adjoining cells.

Alternatively, you can place the epidermis cells in sucrose solution of varying concentrations – 1M, 0.8M, 0.6M, 0.4M, 0.2M and 0M (distilled water). If the

(Continued)

(Continued)

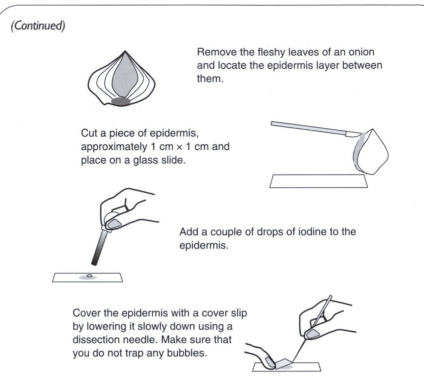

Remove the fleshy leaves of an onion and locate the epidermis layer between them.

Cut a piece of epidermis, approximately 1 cm × 1 cm and place on a glass slide.

Add a couple of drops of iodine to the epidermis.

Cover the epidermis with a cover slip by lowering it slowly down using a dissection needle. Make sure that you do not trap any bubbles.

Figure 1.5   Preparing a plant cell slide

pigment is present then you should be able to see the cell membranes come away from the cell walls as the cells lose water. The cells are said to be plasmolysed if the membranes have detached from the cell wall. This is an alternative experiment to the 'osmosis in potato chips' option (see below).

Diffusion and osmosis

It would be wrong not to mention the processes of diffusion and osmosis when discussing cells. The movement of substances in and out of the cells is vital to the functioning of the cell. Oxygen, water, carbon dioxide, waste and nutrients have to cross the cell membranes to allow life to continue.

Diffusion is the passive movement of molecules or atoms from a high concentration to a low concentration, down what is said to be a concentration gradient. Passive means that no energy is expended by the cell to move that particular substance. Examples of substances that move in and out of cells by diffusion are carbon dioxide, glucose and oxygen. These are generally substances that pass in and out of our blood. This happens quickly as there is no part of the body that is more than a few millimetres away from a blood vessel. This is called a short diffusion distance and is evident in the lungs.

Osmosis is the passive movement of water molecules from a high concentration to a low concentration, across a selectively permeable membrane. It is basically a special type of diffusion that describes how water moves in and out of cells. Students are required to answer exam questions in terms of solute molecules and water molecules. As the solute molecules are too large to pass across the cell membrane, these tend to stay where they are and the smaller water molecules move backwards and forwards. It is useful to tell the students that:

Solvent + Solute = Solution
(e.g. Water + Sugar = Sugar solution)

This makes it easier for the students to understand and then be able to explain the effect of solutes either inside or outside a cell.

Practical activity

Diffusion in jelly cubes

Diffusion and the effect of surface area can be studied by looking at gelatine blocks that contain cresol red – a pH indicator. This is red in alkali conditions and turns yellow when conditions become acidic.

The method is as follows. Start with a gelatine block and cut various cubes using a scalpel. (Care should be taken when using the scalpel.) The sizes should be progressively smaller, and a suitable suggestion is as follows:

- 10 mm × 10 mm × 10 mm
- 10 mm × 10 mm × 5 mm
- 10 mm × 5 mm × 5 mm
- 5 mm × 5 mm × 5 mm

Put the cubes into a test tube, fill the test tube with dilute hydrochloric acid and start a stop watch. Put in a rubber bung and lay the test tube horizontally. Record the time taken for the blocks to change from red to yellow. Use ideas about diffusion and surface-area-to-volume ratio to explain why the smallest cube changes colour first.

Practical activity

Osmosis in potato chips

Osmosis can be studied by cutting potato chips of roughly similar dimensions and then immersing them in varying concentrations of sucrose solution – 1M, 0.8M, 0.6M, 0.4M, 0.2M and 0M (distilled water). Measure the mass of each potato chip before placing it in a boiling tube filled with one of the concentrations suggested. Repeat with the other concentrations of sucrose. Leave for preferably 30 minutes, although reasonable results can be gained after around 20 minutes. Reweigh each chip and calculate the percentage change in mass using the following equation:

$$\frac{\text{Initial mass} - \text{Final mass}}{\text{Initial mass}} \times 100$$

Plotting the results on a graph will allow you to see exactly where the line crosses the origin. This is where the sucrose solution outside the potato cells is the same concentration as the solution inside the cell. This means you can estimate the concentration of the sap inside the potato. The closest value is around 0.4M although this will vary with different potatoes. Encourage the students to feel the chips when they are reweighed. Which chips have gone flaccid (floppy) and which are turgid (hard)?

Water moves out of the cells when the solute concentration outside of the cells is higher than inside. Putting it simply, the sugar concentration outside is higher than the concentration inside of the cell. This means that there is a large concentration gradient and the net movement of water is out of the cells. When there are more water molecules outside (less solute), then there is a net movement of water molecules into the cells.

Engaging activity

It is quite easy to make 3D models using a variety of model making substances, old boxes, string, cotton wool and the like. What makes a more interesting model is an edible model of a cell.

Making a 3D jelly model

Take a plastic container, the kind that you may use to carry sandwiches; this will represent the cell wall. In the box place a variety of different foodstuffs as follows: several grapes representing chloroplasts; several small sweets representing starch grains; one prune/plum or apricot represents a nucleus; several rice crispies represents mitochondria. The actual amounts are not important, but the relative amounts are crucial. For example you only need one nucleus! Mix up some flavoured jelly and pour this into the box. This will need to be refrigerated until set, preferably overnight. The key thing about this is that it gets students to think about cells being three dimensional. They seem confused when they can't see all the contents of a cell under the microscope, without moving the fine focus up and down. Turning the jelly out on to a plate allows you to cut through it to reveal sections, the sort that you might see looking at plant cells using a microscope (see Figure 1.6). This explains why some cells look long and thin while others look equidimensional.

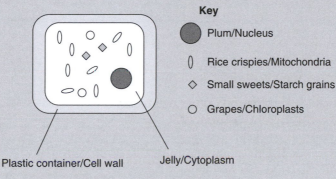

Key

● Plum/Nucleus

◖ Rice crispies/Mitochondria

◇ Small sweets/Starch grains

○ Grapes/Chloroplasts

Plastic container/Cell wall   Jelly/Cytoplasm

Figure 1.6 One slice through the 3D jelly model

Further reading

Kennedy, P. and Sochacki, F. (2008) *Biology AS for OCR*. Oxford: Heinemann Educational. This has useful background information at AS level about cells and cell structure.

Parsons, R. (2003) *GCSE Biology: Complete Revision and Practice*. Kirkby-in-Furness: Co-ordination Group Publications.
This is a useful summary of the level of knowledge required for GCSE.

Parsons, R. (2006) *GCSE Biology, OCR Gateway: The Revision Guide, Higher Level*. Kirkby-in-Furness: Co-ordination Group Publications.
This is a useful summary of the level of knowledge required for GCSE.

2 Human reproduction and genetics

Ruth Richards

This chapter covers:

- ovulation, fertilization and implantation
- the zygote, embryo and foetus
- the menstrual cycle
- the role of the placenta and birth
- DNA structure and extraction
- variation, inheritance and basic genetics.

 Test your own knowledge

Before reading the material in this chapter test your current knowledge with the following questions:

1. What is ovulation and why does it occur?
2. What does the word gamete mean?
3. Put the following in order of size: chromosome, DNA, gene, cell and nucleus.
4. What do the words zygote, embryo and foetus mean?
5. How is sex inherited?

Human reproduction

Although it is not strictly essential for many current specifications, it is useful for students to familiarize themselves with the gross structure of the male and female reproductive systems. Without this the ideas surrounding the rest of the concepts in this chapter lack context. Ensure that the students can label the female genito-urinary parts: ovary, oviduct, uterus, urethra, ureter, bladder, cervix and vagina. They should also be able to label the male genito-urinary parts: testes, scrotum, epididymis, glands (no need to specify), ureter, bladder and urethra. This is a good starting point for this topic and usually stimulates a great deal of discussion because many students have heard of these structures but few can label where they should be.

Ovulation, fertilization and implantation

It is important for students to realize that we all arise originally from one cell – the fertilized egg. The eggs themselves are grown and matured in the ovary of a human female. They find their way out of the ovary during the process of ovulation. This is when the surface of the ovary erupts in response to the mature egg or Graafian follicle pushing its way out of the ovary. Ovulation leaves a small scar on the outside of the ovary. The feathery ends of the oviducts waft the egg into the oviduct itself, where it starts its journey into the uterus. If the egg is fertilized, then it will implant into the wall of the uterus.

Fertilization occurs in the oviducts, not the uterus. If fertilization does not occur, then the lining of the uterus degrades and menstruation occurs. If sperm are ejaculated into the woman's vagina, they will swim up through the uterus towards the egg cell. The egg gives out a chemical signal that draws the sperm in the right direction.

The head of the sperm cell contains a sac containing digestive enzymes which dissolve the outer coat of the egg cell. If a sperm cell and an egg cell then fuse together in the process called fertilization, a zygote or ball of undifferentiated cells is produced. Only one sperm cell penetrates the egg during fertilization. The process of fertilization can be seen in Figure 2.1.

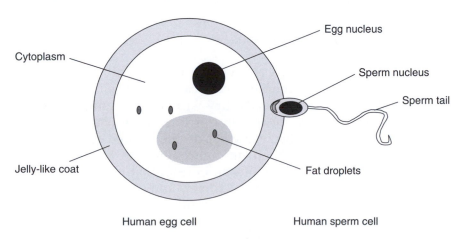

Figure 2.1 Sperm and egg cell during fertilization

In a human there are hormones that stimulate the development of one egg cell (ovum) or follicle. There are eggs at various stages of development in the ovary, but only one develops at a time to become a mature Graafian follicle. It is this follicle that breaks through the external epithelial layer during ovulation. Of course, occasionally there may be more than one egg cell stimulated to grow, resulting in a multiple birth (such as non-identical twins).

Practical activity

Pomegranate model of the ovary

Pomegranates are fruits that are in season from about October to March. A pomegranate can be used to get the students to think about the similarities and differences between the fruit and the ovary in a human female. The pomegranates should be halved prior to starting the activity. The students should consider how good the pomegranate is as a model of the human ovary and should discuss the problems with it. They should compare the similarities and differences between the pomegranate and the human ovary and summarize their findings in groups and then feed back to the whole class.

Pomegranates and ovaries share several things in common in that they have the ability to produce hundreds of eggs or seeds; they have an outer layer keeping everything together; and that not all eggs or seeds are exactly the same size and so may be at different stages of development. The seeds themselves are surrounded by flesh/jelly.

The differences are also clear. Many mature seeds develop at the same time in the pomegranate, which does not happen in a human. The human ovary is about the size of an almond – much smaller than a pomegranate.

The zygote, embryo and foetus

Once the fertilized egg begins to divide, it forms a ball of cells called a zygote. These are undifferentiated cells called stem cells which have not yet decided what type of cells they will be (for example, skin or muscle cells). The position of the head, trunk and legs also needs to start being formed. Once the zygote has decided which cells will start to form which structures, then differentiation has begun and the embryo is formed. Once all the bits and pieces that make up a recognizable human have formed, such as fingers and toes, then the developing baby is called a foetus. A zygote and embryo can be seen in Figure 2.2.

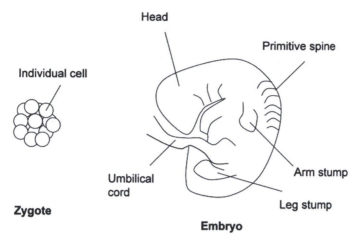

Figure 2.2 An example of a zygote and an embryo

Practical activity

Making a model of a zygote and an embryo

There are many good diagrams on the Internet showing embryonic development in the animal kingdom. Students can use Play Doh or Plasticine to model various stages of their development. If they choose contrasting animals, then a comparison of the models made will reveal where each developing embryo becomes distinctly different.

How science works

Embryonic stem cells can be isolated from the ball of undifferentiated cells that form a zygote. These cells are used in research to develop treatments for a variety of different diseases (for example, neurological diseases). This is because these cells have the potential to develop into any type of cell. This type of research is in its infancy but is constantly in the news and worthy of student discussion – this is a rare opportunity to discuss ethics in class.

Menstrual cycle

The actual process of maturation of the egg cell (ovum) and ovulation is controlled by hormones secreted by the mother. The steps described can

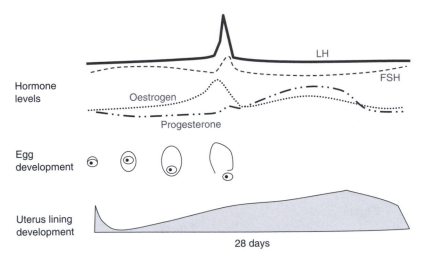

Figure 2.3   The menstrual cycle

be followed by using the information given in Figure 2.3, which shows one female cycle. Follicle-stimulating hormone (FSH) is released from the pituitary gland (brain) into the blood, which stimulates the growth of a follicle (egg) in the ovary. The cells that surround the follicle secrete a hormone from the ovary itself – oestrogen. Oestrogen helps prepare the lining of the uterus to accept implantation from a fertilized egg.

As the follicle becomes bigger, more oestrogen is produced and the lining of the uterus becomes thicker. This increased level of oestrogen in the blood signals the pituitary gland to reduce the level of FSH, as we only want one mature follicle at a time. If this did not occur, then various embryos at different stages of development would be implanted. A peak in the production of oestrogen signals the temporary production of excesses of two hormones from the pituitary gland: luteinizing hormone (LH) and FSH. These have the effect of stimulating ovulation, and then the levels decline rapidly.

The cells in the ovary continue to produce some oestrogen and increased levels of progesterone. The lining of the uterus thickens further to accept a fertilized egg. The combination of oestrogen and progesterone inhibits the production of LH and FSH, thus preventing the development of another follicle. If fertilization does not occur, then the cells in the ovary reduce their production of oestrogen and progesterone. The fall in progesterone means that menstruation is triggered, and so a period starts. The low levels of progesterone mean that FSH is no longer inhibited and the development of a new follicle begins. If fertilization occurs, then the progesterone levels remain high and menstruation is not triggered.

For simplicity, the first half of the cycle is controlled largely by oestrogen and the second by progesterone.

Practical activity

Labelling the menstrual cycle

Taking Figure 2.3 as a basis, annotate the various parts of the cycle using the paragraphs above. Ask the students to draw lines to make links between hormone levels and the effects of these hormones on target areas of the reproductive system (for example, LH and FSH spikes would link to ovulation).

The placenta

The foetus obtains all the nutrients and oxygen it needs to grow through the umbilical cord. This is a structure that links the developing foetus to the placenta. It is not derived from the mother's cells but the cells of the zygote. The placenta itself is a structure found in mammals that allows the exchange of food, oxygen, carbon dioxide and waste. The blood vessels in the uterus are adjacent to those in the placenta, and diffusion occurs between these structures in the same way as it does in the lungs. Only small substances can pass across the placenta, and so it is a barrier to some types of infection.

As the placenta develops it starts to produce progesterone and oestrogen. Increased levels of these hormones are needed to maintain a pregnancy and, after three months' gestation, the placenta produces these hormones taking over the job from the ovary. If the placenta does not produce these hormones, then a healthy pregnancy cannot be maintained and a miscarriage occurs.

Birth

Birth is controlled by a hormone called oxytocin, which is released from the pituitary gland of the foetus. So it is really true that the baby decides when it is ready to be born. During pregnancy the uterus does not become any bigger but it is stretched thinner, rather like a ball of pizza dough becoming a thin pizza base. The hormone causes the contraction of the muscle fibres in the uterus signalling them to shorten, essentially to return to their original shape. This shortening is what causes contractions during labour.

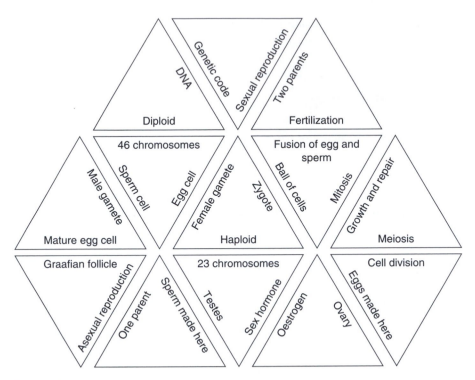

Figure 2.4   Human reproduction jigsaw

The production of oxytocin is an example of positive feedback, so increased levels of the hormone trigger the production of even more of it. Hence the contractions become stronger and the cervix dilates. The later contractions squeeze the baby along the birth canal finally to be born.

The students can test their knowledge of some of the basic terms from this section by completing the jigsaw shown in Figure 2.4.

Deoxyribonucleic acid (DNA)

DNA is the chemical code which controls organisms' characteristics. This genetic code is passed from parent to offspring in both asexual and sexual reproduction. The chemical make-up is relatively simple in DNA, consisting of only four basic units, or nitrogenous base pairs. These are guanine, cytosine, adenine and thymine, or simply G, C, A and T for short. Due to differences in size and a differing number of hydrogen bonds that link the base pairs together, G can only bond with C and A can only bond with T.

DNA is a double strand of base pairs, complementary bonded. It is then twisted to form a double helix or ladder shape which in turn is wound up to form chromosomes in the nucleus of the cell. Chromosomes are thread-like structures that are made of DNA and protein. These are unwound during most of the cell cycle and cannot be seen using a microscope. When the cell is dividing, the DNA shortens and becomes visible when viewed using a microscope.

One analogy to explain this to the students is to describe the unwound chromosomes as spaghetti in a pan and the shortened versions as penne pasta. If you were trying to separate the pasta into two equal piles, it is much easier to separate penne pasta than spaghetti!

It is worth noting that only one half of the DNA strand is the actual genetic information, and this is known as the sense strand. The complementary half does not actually code for anything.

Practical activity

Making DNA models using beads

DNA can be modelled using coloured plastic beads. Collect approximately 500 coloured beads (only four colours are needed to represent the four nitrogenous bases). These should be placed in a bag and two lengths of string should be made available for each student. The beads represent one of the four bases (for example, A = blue, T = green, G = yellow and C = red). The students should construct a key and decide which colour represents which base.

Take both strings and tie one knot at the bottom, keeping the strings relatively taut. Take 21 beads and thread on to one string. Use the other string to thread the complementary bases. A string of beads AATCGA would have the complementary strand as TTAGCT. Thread the complementary pairs on to the second string. Continue until you have all 21 base pairs complete. You have now coded the DNA strand. If you hold the strings tight and twist them, then you will form a double helix. Of course, you could make longer strands if you wish.

This activity can be extended to make the single-stranded mRNA (messenger RNA) and to create protein chains. This can be done by adding an extra colour to represent the base uracil (U), which is present in RNA but not in DNA. U replaces T in mRNA.

Variation, inheritance and genetics

A gene is a section of DNA that controls one characteristic in an organism. Genes are made up of two parts, called alleles. One allele is inherited from your mother and the other from your father. It is these two alleles together that form one gene. Prior to fertilization, each egg cell contains one half of the mother's DNA, and so only one allele for each characteristic. Each sperm contains half of the father's DNA, the second allele for that characteristic. So when they fuse during fertilization, each gene is once again complete: two alleles.

Genes can be dominant or recessive, either expressed or not. Someone may have one recessive allele in a gene but, because they have a dominant allele, the recessive allele is suppressed. Dominant alleles are given capital letters while recessive ones are given lower-case letters.

An example can be shown for rabbits with a brown or black coat colour:

Let B = brown
Let b = black

The possible combinations are BB (brown), bb (black) or Bb (brown because it contains a dominant brown allele). The last combination has two unlike alleles and is called the heterozygous condition. Homozygous means that both alleles are alike.

Two other terms you need to know are as follows:

- **Genotype** – which are the genes an organism contains.
- **Phenotype** – which is the outward expression of the genes (what you see). For example, brown rabbits would look brown.

The monohybrid cross is inheritance of one characteristic (e.g. coat colour). A cross between two heterozygous brown rabbits would be as follows:

Phenotype	Brown mother	Brown father
Genotype	Bb	Bb
Gametes formed (eggs for mother, sperm for father)	B b	B b

The probability square (showing the possibilities for the random fusion of an egg and a sperm) would be as follows:

	B	b
B	BB	Bb
b	Bb	bb

The possible outcomes are:

BB = brown homozygous
Bb = brown heterozygous – there are two of these
Bb = black homozygous

These would be in a ratio of 3:1 (3 = brown; 1 = black).

Inheritance of sex

Sex inheritance follows the same pattern but the chromosomes involved are labelled X and Y. The following combinations are XX = female or XY = male. You have to have two of these chromosomes to develop properly as a human, and one of these has to be an X:

Phenotype	Mother (female)	Father (male)
Genotype	XX	XY
Gametes formed	X X	X Y

The probability square (all the possibilities for the random fusion of an egg and a sperm) would be as follows:

	X	X
X	XX	XX
Y	XY	XY

The possible outcomes are:

XX = female
XY = male

This explains why the numbers of males and females remain fairly constant at a ratio of 1:1 in a society that does not select against one sex or the other.

How science works

The X and Y chromosomes are named such because they resemble these upper-case letters when they are going through the process of meiosis (forming

(Continued)

(Continued)

gametes). The X chromosome is much larger than the Y, containing much more genetic information. The Y chromosome is essentially half an X chromosome.

It is the genes that are present on the X chromosome but absent on the Y chromosome that allow sex-linked diseases (such as colour blindness or haemophilia) to occur. Essentially, the portion of the chromosome (gene) that codes for a feature is absent from the Y chromosome, and so a disease is expressed if it is present on the X chromosome.

Engaging activities

DNA can easily be extracted from kiwi fruits. This is a rather messy practical, but well worth the effort and only uses everyday items, so there is no need for any complex solutions or equipment. The method is as follows.

Extracting the DNA

Measure 50 ml of water into a beaker and add ¼ teaspoon of salt and 1 teaspoon of washing-up liquid. Gently warm the solution to 50 °C. Finely chop half a kiwi fruit and add to the liquid. Stir and then keep the mixture warm for 15 minutes. Take the mixture off the heat and mix in 2 teaspoons of pineapple juice. Liquidize the mixture for about 10 seconds and then strain the solution to get rid of any remaining lumps. Skim off any foam on the surface and discard.

Precipitating the DNA

Pour 10 ml of DNA extract into a beaker. Very carefully add 25 ml of ice-cold alcohol down the side of the glass. The alcohol should form a layer on the top of the mixture. The interface between the mixture and the alcohol is where you should begin to see white threads forming. This may take several minutes to form.

You can look at the DNA in your own cells but this requires you to take a sample of your own cheek cells (epithelial cells). Follow the same method to remove the cheek cells using a scraper as was described in Chapter 1. The students quite like this as they are looking at their own DNA, and this method yields visible strands if the students are patient.

Further reading

Parsons, R. (2005) *A2 Level Biology*. Kirkby-in-Furness: Co-ordination Group Publications. Contains a useful, well explained section on meiosis to enhance subject knowledge and a useful section on genetics.

Toole, G. and Toole, S. (2004) *Essential A2 Biology*. Cheltenham: Nelson Thornes. A useful summary of both sexual reproduction and genetics.

http://home.honolulu.hawaii.edu/~pine/book1qts/embryo-compare.jpg
Shows the development of various animals, such as chickens, rabbits and humans, in embryonic form.

www.cellsalive.com/mitosis.htm
Shows a useful animation of mitosis and meiosis.

Section 2

Chemical and material properties

In this section, of four chapters, you will be introduced to the science of:

- separating materials;
- endothermic and exothermic reactions;
- reactivity and the reactivity series; and
- acids and bases.

This links to, and will help you deliver, the various national curricula for England, Ireland, Scotland and Wales as set out below.

By working through this section it is expected that you will be able to describe and explain:

- various methods of separating mixtures;
- both endothermic and exothermic reactions;
- the reactivity series; and
- acids, alkalis and bases.

Please turn over to see how this section relates to your curriculum.

National Curriculum for England	Junior Certificate Science Syllabus	Environmental Studies – Society, Science and Technology	Science in the National Curriculum for Wales
KS3 Elements and compounds show characteristic chemical properties and patterns in their behaviour **AT3** Materials and their properties: … using appropriate technology, for example separation methods **KS4** **6a** Chemical change takes place by the rearrangement of atoms in substances **6b** There are patterns in the chemical reactions between substances **6c** New materials are made from natural resources by chemical reactions	**2A4** Metals: properties, of metals **2C4** Metals: relative reactivities of Ca, Mg, Zn and Cu **2A2** Mixtures: separating substances using filtration, evaporation, distillation and paper chromatography **2A7** Water and solutions: water as a solvent **2C3** Rusting and corrosion: rusting as a chemical process **2C5** Hydrocarbons: products of combustion of fossil fuels	Changing materials: Describe what happens when metals react with oxygen, water and acids Describe how metal elements can be extracted from compounds in the Earth's crust Changing materials: Distinguish between soluble and insoluble materials Explain how evaporation and filtration can be used in the separation of solids from liquids Materials from Earth: Give examples of useful materials that we obtain from the Earth's crust Changing materials: Describe changes when materials are mixed Give examples of simple chemical reactions, explaining them in terms of elements and compounds Give examples of chemical reactions using word equations	**KS3** Materials and their properties: **1** Classifying materials (**10** separating mixtures into their constituents) **2** Changing materials (**10** chemical reactions) **3** Patterns of behaviour (**1–4** metals) **KS4** Materials and their properties: **2** Patterns of behaviour (**8** the periodic table) Changing materials: **2** Physical changes (**2** solutes have different solubilities in different solvents) **KS4** Materials and their properties: **2** Patterns of behaviour (**15–17** energy transfer in reactions)

3 Separating materials

John Twidle

This chapter covers:

- extracting iron from cornflakes and salt from beneath the ground
- chromatography
- gas chromatography
- simple distillation.

 Test your own knowledge

Before reading the material in this chapter test your current knowledge with the following questions:

1. How do breakfast cereal manufacturers produce a product that is *enriched with iron?*
2. Why does eating spinach not provide you with as much iron as you might think?
3. Design a method to extract a mineral from underground that is beneath a sandy soil that would make it unsafe to mine in a conventional way.
4. How you would test to see if two different sweets contained the same dyes?
5. Why does it matter which way the water flows in a Liebig condenser?

Common ways of separating materials in the laboratory include mechanical methods, dissolving, filtering, chromatography and distillation. These methods have important uses in everyday life and industry.

Mechanical methods

A traditional method of demonstrating that a combination of iron filings and sulphur can be separated before they are heated and that they cannot after they have been heated and a chemical reaction has taken place is to pick up the iron filings with a magnet. However, iron filings are found in some unexpected places and can be separated in the same way.

Engaging activity

Extracting iron from cornflakes

Iron and its compounds are an important part of our diet because they are essential for the production of haemoglobin. Manufacturers enrich many foods (such as flour, 'Special K' and cornflakes) with iron which reacts with the hydrochloric acid in the stomach before being absorbed in the intestines. Iron metal is used instead of iron compounds because it does not react with any other ingredients in the foodstuff and has no taste.

Apparatus

For this activity you will need the following equipment:

- Safety spectacles
- A pestle and mortar
- A strong neodymium magnet
- A sheet of paper
- A supply of breakfast cereal containing added iron (check the label)
- Either 2 M hydrochloric acid or 1 M sulphuric acid
- Potassium hexacyanoferrate(III) solution
- A test tube and rack

Method

Grind a few breakfast cereal flakes to a fine powder with the pestle and mortar and tip the powder on to a clean sheet of paper. Place the neodymium magnet on the bench beneath the paper and move the paper over the magnet. With care, it is possible to isolate a few fine grey specks of iron from the rest of the cereal.

It is possible to show that the grey powder is iron by reacting it with 2 M hydrochloric acid to produce iron(II) chloride and hydrogen. An alternative method would be to use 1 M sulphuric acid but, since hydrochloric acid is present in the human stomach, this would seem more appropriate. When a few drops of potassium hexacyanoferrate(III) solution are added to the iron(II) chloride solution, a dark blue precipitate is produced.

Popeye the Sailor was mistaken

The myth that spinach is high in iron comes from a simple mistake – the recording of a number with the decimal point in the wrong place. It gave spinach the reputation of having 10 times more iron than any other green vegetable. Not only does spinach have one tenth of the iron many believe it to have but there is also another problem – spinach contains traces of oxalic acid which renders the iron insoluble and difficult to absorb.

Dissolving

The students would probably have encountered the traditional problem of separating salt from sand early on in their science careers. However, the following practical activity gives them a challenge that reminds them of, and draws upon, the principles used in that process.

Engaging activity

Extracting salt from beneath the ground

The students will probably be familiar with the fact that salt can be obtained by evaporating sea water but may not be aware that layers of salt are also found underneath the ground in England. Deposits of salt are often found mixed in with layers of sand which would collapse if the salt were to be mined, so a different method of extraction has to be used.

Note: The model salt mines referred to below need to be prepared in advance and one given to each student or group of students.

Apparatus

For this activity you will need the following equipment:

- Safety spectacles
- A 250 cm³ beaker
- A plastic lemonade bottle with a layer of salt at the bottom, covered with layers of sand and stones (a small lemonade bottle would present an easier task than a 2 litre version)
- Plastic tubes
- Blu-Tack or Plasticine
- Filter paper and a funnel
- An evaporating basin
- A tripod, gauze, Bunsen burner and heatproof mat

(Continued)

(Continued)

Method

The students are presented with the lemonade bottle as a model of the salt deposits and given the challenge of obtaining a pure sample of salt from the bottle. They are not, however, allowed to tip the contents out or to invert the bottle.

Hint: Feeding a plastic tube down through the layers of sand and stones allows water to be fed down into the salt layer to dissolve the salt. A second tube will allow the salt solution to be brought to the surface, which can then be filtered to remove the sand and evaporated to leave clean salt. A less imaginative student might be allowed to pour off the salt solution that rises to the surface of the sand and stones but it is a greater challenge if that strategy is not allowed.

Chromatography

Chromatography is used to separate mixtures into their components and all forms of chromatography work on the same principle. They all have a stationary phase (a solid) and a mobile phase (liquid or gas). The mobile phase travels through the stationary phase and carries the mixture with it. Different components of the mixture travel at different rates.

R_f values

Some components of a mixture travel almost as far as the solvent does and some hardly move at all. The distance a material travels relative to the solvent is constant (as long as the conditions are constant). The distance travelled relative to the solvent front is called the R_f value and can be worked out using the formula:

$$R_f = \frac{\text{Distance travelled by compound}}{\text{Distance travelled by solvent}}$$

For example, if one component of a mixture travelled 8.0 cm from the pencil base-line and the solvent travelled 12.0 cm, then the R_f value for that component is:

$$R_f = \frac{8.0}{12.0} = 0.75$$

In paper chromatography, samples of inks, for example, are spotted on to a pencil line drawn on a sheet of chromatography paper. It is important that the base-line is drawn in pencil as it is insoluble in the different solvents and does not move. The paper is suspended in a container of a suitable solvent so that the ink spots are above the surface of the solvent. As the solvent rises up the paper, the different components of the ink travel at different rates and the mixtures are separated into different-coloured spots.

Practical activity

The chromatography of M&Ms

In order to make chromatography more relevant to the students, they can use the technique to separate the different dyes used in sweets.

Apparatus

For this activity you will need the following equipment:

- A 250 cm^3 beaker
- Chromatography paper (or rectangles cut from filter paper as a substitute)
- A pencil and ruler
- A splint
- Paper clips
- A small artist's paintbrush
- A hair dryer or fan heater
- A supply of M&M sweets (not the peanut variety in order to avoid the possibility of a student having a severe allergic reaction). The chromatography of Smarties is less successful because they contain natural food colourings.

Method

Draw a horizontal pencil line across the chromatography paper about 2 cm up from the base. Dampen the paintbrush and use it to remove a sample of one of the dyes from the surface of one of the M&Ms. Transfer the dye to a spot on the line drawn on the chromatography paper about 2 cm from the edge. Dry the spot by blowing warm air across it with the hair dryer or fan. Repeat the process to build up a concentration of the dye on the same spot.

Using the same process, transfer other colours to build up spots 2 cm apart along the line. Label the coloured spots (in pencil).

(Continued)

(Continued)

Add water to the beaker up to a depth of about 1 cm. Attach the chromatography paper to the splint with paper clips and suspend it in the beaker so that the pencil line is about 1 cm above the surface of the water, as in Figure 3.1. Leave the apparatus for 5–10 minutes so that the solvent and dyes have risen sufficiently far up the chromatography paper.

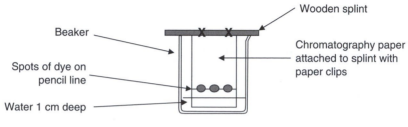

Figure 3.1   Chromatography of dyes from sweets

Engaging activity

The chromatography of grass

As an alternative to the chromatography of the dyes in sweets and as an introduction to photosynthesis, the experiment can be carried out with the juice from green plants.

Apparatus

For this activity you will need the following equipment:

- A pestle and mortar
- A 250 cm³ beaker
- Chromatography paper (or rectangles cut from filter paper as a substitute)
- A pencil and ruler
- A splint
- Paper clips
- A pipette
- A hair dryer or fan heater
- Green leaves, such as grass or spinach
- Ethanol
- Sand

Method

Tear up a few blades of grass or spinach leaves and add them to the pestle and mortar. Add a few drops of ethanol and a pinch of sand to the leaves and grind them to form a green slurry.

Prepare a sheet of chromatography paper as in the M&Ms experiment and transfer a drop of the green slurry to a spot on the pencil line. As before, try to build up a spot of intense colour by adding a series of drops of the mixture and drying the chromatography paper with the hair dryer or fan between the drops added.

Run the chromatogram as before but using ethanol as the solvent. It might be helpful to cover the beaker with cling film to reduce the loss of solvent by evaporation.

As might be expected, a green spot moves up the paper but an orange/yellow spot also separates out that belongs to a group of pigments called carotenoids that absorb light of a different wavelength from chlorophyll.

Gas chromatography

Gas chromatography is a widely used method for the analysis of volatile components in sample mixtures. In commercial gas chromatographs, the mobile carrier is an inert gas, such as helium, and the stationary phase is an inert solid held in a length of tube. Samples for analysis are fed into the carrier gas at one end of the tube and the different components pass through the tube at different rates. As the different components of the mixture leave the tube they are detected by a suitable detector (live male insects have even been used to detect insect pheromones). The samples analysed can be solids, liquids or gases but solids or liquids must be turned into a gas before they will work.

Practical activity

A demonstration of gas chromatography

A simple demonstration gas chromatograph model can be made from a length of glass tubing filled with sodium tripolyphosphate – which is found in several washing powders – as the stationary phase, and by using natural gas (methane) as the carrier. The methane leaving the chromatograph is burnt and, as each component leaves the tube, it causes a fluctuation in the flame.

(Continued)

(Continued)

Apparatus

For this activity you will need the following equipment:

- A demonstration gas chromatograph
- A hypodermic syringe
- Samples of volatile organic compounds
- A stopwatch

Method

Arrange the gas chromatograph as shown in Figure 3.2. Turn on the supply of natural gas and allow it to run for a few seconds before igniting the gas as it exits the burette jet.

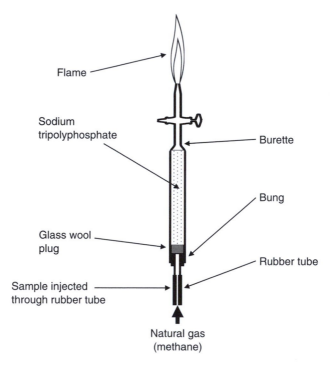

Flame

Sodium tripolyphosphate

Burette

Bung

Glass wool plug

Rubber tube

Sample injected through rubber tube

Natural gas (methane)

Figure 3.2   Gas chromatography

Using the hypodermic syringe (with care), draw a sample of the vapour from above the volatile solvent. Using the hypodermic syringe, carefully inject the sample of vapour through the rubber tube feeding the burette and note how long it takes for the flame to fluctuate.

Purge the syringe several times with air before filling it with a different vapour and compare the difference in time it takes the flame to fluctuate. Repeat the process using a mix of the different vapours.

Distillation

In simple distillation (as seen in Figure 3.3) liquids, such as water, can be separated from a dissolved solid, such as salt. In fractional distillation, a mixture of liquids with different boiling points can be separated by heating.

During the process, it is important that the thermometer's bulb is level with the outlet of the distillation flask, where it should register the temperature of the boiling point of the liquid being distilled off. For example, if a mixture of salt and water is being used, then the temperature should read 100°C – the boiling point of pure water at normal atmospheric pressure. However, if the thermometer's bulb were to be placed in the salt solution below, the temperature would be much higher.

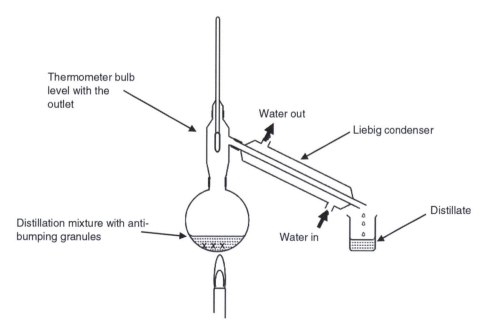

Figure 3.3 Simple distillation

It is also important to add a few pieces of broken porcelain, or commercial anti-bumping granules, to the liquid being distilled to give the bubbles of steam a surface to form around. If anti-bumping granules are not used, then there is a danger that the liquid may boil suddenly and unpredictably. This is called bump boiling. Similarly, if a drink is heated up in a microwave oven in a cup with a very smooth surface, then it is possible to heat the contents up to well above their normal boiling point (superheated). Once a spoon of coffee or sugar is added to the drink this gives the bubbles of steam a surface to form around, resulting in the liquid all boiling at once and spraying over your hand. It is safer to add a spoon of coffee powder to the liquid before placing it in the microwave.

It is similarly important that the cooling water flows in the direction indicated in Figure 3.3 so that efficient cooling can take place. Not only does the cold water cool down and condense the hot gases but the hot gases also heat up the cooling water. If the water flows in the opposite direction, then it will be warmer by the time it flows out of the condenser and will not cool down the condensed gases as efficiently. Although the water in the outer jacket will still be warmed up when it flows in the 'correct' direction (as shown in Figure 3.3), it can still cool down the much hotter gases leaving the distillation flask.

Further reading

McDuell, B. (2000) *Teaching Secondary Chemistry*. London: John Murray.

Ryan, L. (2006) *New Chemistry for You*. Cheltenham: Nelson Thornes.
These are two general chemistry texts that cover a broad spectrum of GCSE topics.

www.eatwell.gov.uk/healthydiet/nutritionessentials/vitaminsand minerals/iron/
The website of the Food Standards Agency, where further information on the absorption of iron from food can be found.

4 Exothermic and endothermic reactions

John Twidle

This chapter covers:

- different examples of exothermic and endothermic reactions
- everyday uses of exothermic and endothermic reactions
- calculations on energy changes during a chemical reaction.

Test your own knowledge

Before reading the material in this chapter test your current knowledge with the following questions:

1. Give everyday examples of where exothermic and endothermic reactions are useful.
2. Name the type of reaction when an acid and an alkali react. Give an example and write word and symbol equations for the reaction.
3. Name and give an example of the type of reaction when a metal takes the place of a less reactive metal in a chemical reaction.
4. What sort of energy changes take place during the breaking of existing chemical bonds and the making of new ones?

Exothermic and endothermic

When a chemical reaction takes place, as well as forming new products, there is a change in energy, and this change in energy can be detected as a change in temperature. If the products contain less energy than the reactants, then energy is transferred to the surroundings and the reaction is called an exothermic reaction. If the products contain more energy than the reactants, then energy is absorbed from the surroundings and the reaction is called an endothermic reaction.

Practical activity

Introducing exothermic and endothermic reactions

Apparatus

For this activity you will need the following equipment:

- Safety spectacles
- A −10°C to +110°C stirring thermometer
- Boiling tubes and test-tube rack
- A 10 cm^3 measuring cylinder
- A spatula

You will also need access to 0.4 M solutions of:

- Copper(II) sulphate
- Hydrochloric acid
- Sodium hydrogencarbonate
- Sodium hydroxide
- Sulphuric acid

And access to:

- Citric acid
- Iron filings
- Magnesium ribbon cut into 3 cm lengths

Method

Measure out 10 cm^3 of the hydrochloric acid with the measuring cylinder and pour it into a boiling tube. Measure and record the temperature of the acid. Measure out 10 cm^3 of the sodium hydroxide solution and add this to the acid in the boiling tube. Stir the mixture with the thermometer and record the new temperature. Work out the change in temperature and record if the reaction is exothermic or endothermic (exothermic).

   Measure out 10 cm^3 of the sulphuric acid with the measuring cylinder and pour it into a boiling tube. Measure and record the temperature of the acid. Add a 3 cm strip of magnesium ribbon to the acid. Stir the mixture with the thermometer and record the new temperature. Work out the change in temperature and record if the reaction is exothermic or endothermic (exothermic).

Measure out 10 cm³ of the copper(II) sulphate solution with the measuring cylinder and pour it into a boiling tube. Measure and record the temperature of the solution. Add a spatula of iron filings to the solution. Stir the mixture with the thermometer and record the new temperature. Work out the change in temperature and record if the reaction is exothermic or endothermic (exothermic).

Measure out 10 cm³ of the sodium hydrogencarbonate solution with the measuring cylinder and pour it into a boiling tube. Measure and record the temperature of the solution. Add a spatula of citric acid to the solution. Stir the mixture with the thermometer and record the new temperature. Work out the change in temperature and record if the reaction is exothermic or endothermic (endothermic).

Notes

The reactions and types of reactions are as follows:

Neutralization

Word equation	Sodium hydroxide	+	Hydrochloric acid	→	Sodium chloride	+	Water
Symbol equation	NaOH (aq)	+	HCl (aq)	→	NaCl (aq)	+	H_2O (l)

Displacement

Word equation	Sulphuric acid	+	Magnesium	→	Magnesium sulphate	+	Hydrogen
Symbol equation	H_2SO_4 (aq)	+	Mg (s)	→	$MgSO_4$ (aq)	+	H_2 (g)

Displacement

Word equation	Copper(II) sulphate	+	Iron	→	Iron(II) sulphate	+	Copper
Symbol equation	$CuSO_4$ (aq)	+	Fe (s)	→	$FeSO_4$ (aq)	+	Cu (s)

Neutralization

(*Note:* The symbol equation is too complex for GCSE level, so it would be advisable to limit the equation to the word equation)

Word equation	Sodium hydrogen carbonate	+	Citric acid	→	Sodium citrate	+	Carbon dioxide	+	Water

Plaster of Paris disaster

Plaster of Paris is commonly used for casts to support broken bones and to pour into rubber moulds to make a variety of ornaments. When plaster of Paris sets, a strongly exothermic reaction takes place between it and water. When a cast is made for a broken bone, the plaster layer is quite thin and heat energy passes harmlessly into the atmosphere.

A student decided to make a cast of her hands and placed them into a container of plaster of Paris mixture. When the plaster was setting, it released a great deal of energy, which could not easily be transferred to the atmosphere, and a temperature of around 150°C was achieved. Since the girl's hands were embedded in the plaster she was unable to remove them, with the result that her fingers were so badly burnt that several of them had to be amputated.

Plaster of Paris is the common name for calcium sulphate, which originally came from quarries in Montmartre, a region of Paris.

The following two activities show endothermic and exothermic reactions quite dramatically.

Engaging activity

Endothermic reaction between hydrated barium hydroxide and ammonium salts

Mixing two dry solids, barium hydroxide and either of two ammonium salts, demonstrates an endothermic reaction. The odour of ammonia is noticeable, as is the formation of a liquid, and the flask becomes cold. Within a minute or two, the temperature of the mixture drops to well below freezing.

Apparatus

For this activity you will need the following equipment:

- 32 g barium hydroxide octahydrate, $Ba(OH)_2.8H_2O$
- 11 g ammonium chloride, NH_4Cl, or 17 g ammonium nitrate, NH_4NO_3
- A 250 cm^3 conical flask
- A −38°C to +50°C thermometer (optional)
- A small block of wood, approximately 15 cm × 15 cm × 2 cm
- Cling film

Method

Place the pre-weighed amounts of solid barium hydroxide and one of the ammonium salts in the conical flask. Cover the flask with cling film to reduce the ammonia escaping and shake gently to mix the reagents. Within about 30 seconds the flask will become cold to the touch. The temperature will drop to about −25°C or −30° C within 1–2 minutes and will remain below −20°C for several minutes. Pass the flask around the class but warn the students not to touch it for more than a few seconds.

The temperature can be measured directly using the thermometer. In addition, wet the small wooden block with a few drops of water and set the reaction flask on it. The flask will quickly freeze to the block and both can be lifted together off the table.

Hazards

This reaction produces temperatures much lower than body temperature, so the flask should be handled with care and prolonged contact with the skin should be avoided.

Soluble barium salts are toxic if ingested. Upon contact with skin, barium and ammonium salts may produce minor irritation or allergic reactions. If the flask is spilled or broken, its contents should be flushed down the drain with water.

The inhalation of concentrated ammonia vapour causes oedema of the respiratory tract. Seek medical advice.

Disposal

The contents of the flask can be flushed down the drain with water.

Equations

Word equation	Hydrated barium hydroxide	+	Ammonium nitrate	→	Barium nitrate	+	Ammonia	+	Water

Symbol equation $Ba(OH)_2.8H_2O$ (s) + $2NH_4NO_3$ (s) → $Ba(NO_3)_2$ (s) + $2NH_3$ (aq) + $10H_2O$ (l)

Word equation	Hydrated barium hydroxide	+	Ammonium chloride	→	Barium chloride	+	Ammonia	+	Water

Symbol equation $Ba(OH)_2.8H_2O$ (s) + $2NH_4Cl$ (s) → $BaCl_2.2H_2O$ (s) + $2NH_3$ (aq) + $8H_2O$ (l)

Engaging activity

Exothermic reaction: heat of solution of lithium chloride

In this activity, aqueous lithium and chloride ions are formed and the temperature rises to about 65 °C above room temperature.

(Continued)

(Continued)

Apparatus

For this activity you will need the following equipment.

- 42 g of lithium chloride, LiCl
- 50 cm³ distilled water
- Two polystyrene cups
- A thermometer, −10°C to +110°C

Method

Place the two cups inside each other. Place 42 g of lithium chloride in the inner cup and add 50 cm³ of distilled water. Stir and measure the temperature. The temperature will increase to about 65 °C above room temperature.

Equation

Word equation	Lithium chloride solid	$\rightarrow$	Aqueous lithium ions	+	Aqueous chloride ions
Symbol equation	LiCl (s)	$\rightarrow$	Li$^+$ (aq)	+	Cl$^-$ (aq)

Hazards

The reaction produces sufficient heat to cause burns.

Disposal

The solution should be flushed down the drain with water.

In everyday life, many reactions that the students will be familiar with will be exothermic, such as burning fossil fuels to release heat energy or the reactions that take place within the cells of our own bodies to release energy for life. It is far more uncommon for reactions to be used to absorb energy from their surroundings, and industrial reactions that are endothermic are, more often than not, seen to be challenges to be overcome or minimized. However, the following endothermic reaction may well be one that the students are familiar with.

Practical activity

Dissolving ammonium salts in water

Apparatus

For this activity you will need the following equipment:

- A polystyrene cup
- Water

- A 250cm³ beaker
- A stirring rod
- 100 g ammonium nitrate
- A −10°C to +110°C stirring thermometer
- A 100 cm³ measuring cylinder

Method

Measure out 100 cm³ water with the measuring cylinder and pour it into the polystyrene cup. The polystyrene cup will fit neatly inside the 250 cm³ beaker and will prevent it from toppling over.

Measure the temperature of the water. Add the ammonium nitrate to the water and stir the mixture with the stirring rod until it dissolves. Record the temperature of the solution, which should drop below 0°C.

Equation

Word equation	Ammonium nitrate	+	Water	→	Aqueous ammonium ions	+	Aqueous nitrate ions
Symbol equation	NH_4NO_3 (s)	+	H_2O (l)	→	NH_4^+ (aq)	+	NO_3^- (aq)

Similar reactions take place when ammonium chloride or urea are dissolved in water.

These reactions form the basis of the commercial ice packs that are used to treat minor sports injuries. Inside a tough outer plastic bag there are small amounts of ammonium nitrate, ammonium chloride or urea which are separated from a quantity of water by a thin membrane. When the pack is struck with the palm of the hand, the membrane is broken and the contents dissolve in the water. Since the reactions are endothermic, they absorb heat from their surroundings, and the ice pack will maintain a temperature around freezing point for 20–30 minutes.

Energy diagrams, bond energies and the heat of reaction

Energy diagrams

During chemical reactions, two stages take place. First, any existing bonds have to be broken, followed by the forming of new bonds. Breaking existing bonds requires energy to be put into the system (endothermic), and making new bonds involves the release of energy into the surroundings (exothermic). The energy that has to be put into a system to break any

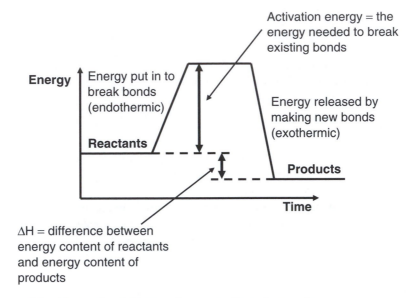

Figure 4.1 Energy-level diagram for an exothermic reaction

existing bonds is called the activation energy. These stages of a chemical reaction can be represented by an energy diagram (see Figure 4.1).

In the reaction shown in Figure 4.1, more energy is released when new bonds are made than has to be provided to break existing bonds. The difference between the energy level of the reactants and the energy level of the products is referred to as the heat of reaction and has the symbol ΔH (measured in Joules). In this case, the reaction is exothermic and ΔH is negative (–ve). For an endothermic reaction, ΔH would be positive (+ve) and the energy level diagram would have the energy level of the products higher than that of the reactants, as can be seen in Figure 4.2.

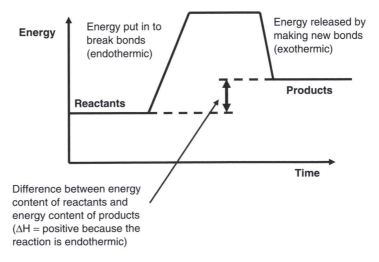

Figure 4.2 Energy-level diagram for an endothermic reaction

Bond energies

In Table 4.1, the bond energy is the energy (in Joules) either absorbed or released when one mole of the bonds is either broken or formed.

Example 1

Calculate the amount of energy released when 1 mole of hydrogen is burnt in chlorine. The symbol equation for the reaction is:

$$H_2 + Cl_2 \rightarrow 2HCl$$

But think of the reaction as:

$$H—H + Cl—Cl \rightarrow H—Cl + H—Cl$$

The energy needed to break bonds is:

$$436 + 242 = 678 \text{ kJ } (+678 \text{ kJ as the chemicals gain energy})$$

The energy released when new bonds are formed is:

$$431 + 431 = 862 \text{ kJ } (-862 \text{ kJ as energy is given out})$$

The net difference between the two stages is:

$$678 - 862 = -184 \text{ kJ per mole of hydrogen burnt (the reaction is exothermic)}$$

Table 4.1   Bond energies

Bond	Bond energy in kJ per mole
H—H	436
H—Cl	431
Cl—Cl	242
O—H	464
O==O	498
C—H	413
C==O	805
N—H	391

Example 2

Calculate the amount of energy released when 1 mole of methane is burnt in oxygen. The symbol equation for the reaction is:

$$CH_4 + 2O_2 \rightarrow CO_2 + 2H_2O$$

But think of the reaction as:

The energy needed to break bonds is:

$$4 \times 413 + 2 \times 498$$
$$= 1652 + 996$$
$$= 2648 \text{ kJ} \ (+2648 \text{ kJ as the chemicals gain energy})$$

The energy released when the new bonds are formed is:

$$2 \times 805 + 2 \times 2 \times 464$$
$$= 1610 + 1856$$
$$= 3466 \text{ kJ} \ (-3466 \text{ kJ as energy is given out})$$

The net difference between the two stages is:

$$2648 - 3466 = -818 \text{ kJ per mole of methane burnt (the reaction is}$$
exothermic)

Further reading

Jones, A., Clemmet, M., Higton, A. and Golding, E. (1999) *Access to Chemistry*. Cambridge: Royal Society of Chemistry.
   This is a good study guide that prepares the reader for A-level chemistry courses or those of an equivalent standing.

Ryan, L. (2006) *New Chemistry for You*. Cheltenham: Nelson Thornes.
   A general chemistry text that covers a broad spectrum of GCSE chemistry topics.

Shakhashiri, B.Z. (1983) *Chemical Demonstrations 1: A Handbook for Teachers of Chemistry*. Madison, WI: University of Winsconsin Press.
   This contains a series of impressive thermochemistry demonstrations.

5 The reactivity series
John Twidle and Mark Crowley

This chapter covers:

- metals reacting with oxygen, water and acids
- displacement reactions
- extracting metals
- simple cells.

Test your own knowledge

Before reading the material in this chapter test your current knowledge with the following questions:

1. Is it possible to predict how a metal will react from its position in the reactivity series?
2. Why can a food can's protective coating sometimes do more harm than good?
3. How can a block of magnesium stop a ship rusting away?
4. How can a reactive metal be extracted with an electric current?

Metals and reactivity

Metals have varying degrees of reactivity, ranging from explosive when added to water to having no reaction at all even with the most corrosive of acids. Common metals can be placed in an order of reactivity (see Table 5.1) called the reactivity series.

Table 5.1   *Reactivity series*

Metal	Symbol
Potassium	K
Sodium	Na
Calcium	Ca
Magnesium	Mg
Aluminium	Al
Zinc	Zn
Iron	Fe
Tin	Sn
Lead	Pb
Copper	Cu
Silver	Ag
Gold	Au

The higher the metal is in the reactivity series, the more reactive it is (i.e. the faster it reacts with oxygen, water and acids and the more exothermic the reaction).

When metals react, what happens – at an atomic level – is that they lose electrons to form positive ions. For example, when potassium reacts with water each atom loses an electron to become a potassium ion with a single positive charge:

Word equation   Potassium + Water → Potassium hydroxide + Hydrogen

Symbol equation $2K (s) + 2H_2O (l) → 2KOH (aq) + H_2 (g)$

What happens to potassium $K → K^+ + e^-$

Similarly, when magnesium reacts with dilute sulphuric acid, each atom loses two electrons to become a magnesium ion with a double positive charge:

Word equation   Magnesium + Sulphuric acid → Magnesium sulphate + Hydrogen

Symbol equation $Mg (s) + H_2SO_4 (aq) → MgSO_4 (aq) + H_2 (g)$

What happens to magnesium $Mg → Mg^{2+} + 2e^-$

When metals are extracted from their ores, these reactions are reversed and metal ions gain electrons to become metal atoms. It follows that the more reactive a metal is, the more difficult it is to reverse this reaction and, therefore, the more difficult it is to extract the metal.

The reactivity series can be established by a range of reactions, such as the metals' reactions, with oxygen, water and acids, and by displacement reactions.

Practical activity

Metals reacting with oxygen

The more reactive metals, such as potassium, sodium and lithium, will react rapidly when exposed to oxygen in the air and, for this reason, are stored in oil. Great care in handling the metals is needed as they form strong, corrosive alkalis in contact with even the moisture on skin. The alkalis formed feel slippery to the touch because they react with fat in the skin to convert it to soap.

All three metals are extremely soft and can be cut with a sharp scalpel. The moment the protective layer of oil is blotted off, the metals begin to react visibly with oxygen in the air: lithium starts to tarnish and loses its lustre after 15–20 seconds, sodium after 10–15 seconds and potassium almost instantly.

It would be unwise to burn these metals in oxygen but those metals slightly lower in the reactivity series will burn readily in oxygen (demonstrations only).

Calcium

For a demonstration, place a fresh turning of calcium on a burning spoon and heat one corner of the turning strongly with a Bunsen flame. When the turning starts to burn, lower it into a gas jar of oxygen. The calcium will burn quickly in the oxygen with a brick red flame to form white calcium oxide:

Word equation	Calcium	+	Oxygen	$\rightarrow$	Calcium oxide
Symbol equation	$2Ca\ (s)$	+	$O_2\ (g)$	$\rightarrow$	$2CaO\ (s)$

Smelly calcium

Pupils often have the impression that the nitrogen in the air is unreactive and that it is only the oxygen involved in burning. However, upon standing for a long time, calcium metal will react with nitrogen in the air to form calcium nitride. The calcium nitride then reacts with any moisture present, resulting in the release of

(Continued)

(Continued)

ammonia gas which can be tested for by either its smell (caution) or it turning damp red litmus blue.

Magnesium

In a similar reaction to calcium, when lowered into a gas jar of oxygen, a short length of burning magnesium ribbon will burn with a brilliant white flame (care is needed and pupils should avoid looking directly at the flame), forming white magnesium oxide.

Word equation   Magnesium   +   Oxygen   →   Magnesium oxide

Symbol equation $2Mg\ (s)$ + $O_2\ (g)$ → $2MgO\ (s)$

When water is added to the oxides formed in these reactions, the metal oxides dissolve and form the alkaline metal hydroxides.

Word equation   Magnesium oxide   +   Water   →   Magnesium hydroxide

Symbol equation $2MgO\ (s)$ + $H_2O\ (l)$ → $2Mg(OH)_2\ (aq)$

An extension activity

When burning magnesium is plunged into a gas jar of carbon dioxide gas, it continues to burn and black specks are formed. More able pupils could be set the challenge of finding an explanation for this phenomenon. (The burning magnesium removes oxygen from the carbon dioxide gas and leaves specks of black carbon.)

Aluminium

Although aluminium metal is reactive and forms a surface layer of white aluminium oxide when heated, the oxide layer protects the aluminium underneath from further reaction and so it appears that the aluminium has not reacted:

Word equation   Aluminium   +   Oxygen   →   Aluminium oxide

Symbol equation $4Al\ (s)$ + $3O_2\ (g)$ → $2Al_2O_3\ (s)$

This protective oxide layer forms on the aluminium when left exposed to the air and is the dirty-white surface seen on TV aerials and greenhouse frames. This explains why aluminium structures last longer than similar iron ones even though aluminium is a more reactive metal. The aluminium oxide layer is so thin that it can be transparent, meaning that the metal underneath still appears shiny silver. Some manufacturers of aluminium products deliberately form the oxide as a protective layer by making it the anode in an electrolysis cell (anodizing) and then dyeing the freshly formed layer to give a decorative effect.

Zinc

When zinc is heated, a similar protective layer of white zinc oxide is formed. A curious property of zinc oxide is that it is yellow when hot but turns white on cooling:

Word equation	Zinc	+	Oxygen	$\rightarrow$	Zinc oxide
Symbol equation	$2Zn$ (s)	+	O_2 (g)	$\rightarrow$	$2ZnO$ (s)

Iron

The surface of iron turns black when heated strongly in air to form tri-iron tetroxide (diron(III)iron(II) oxide):

Word equation	Iron	+	Oxygen	$\rightarrow$	diron(III)iron(II) oxide
Symbol equation	$3Fe$ (s)	+	$2O_2$ (g)	$\rightarrow$	Fe_3O_4 (s)

This reaction is much faster if iron wool is used instead of a large lump of iron. If a small ball of iron wool is heated on a burning spoon in a Bunsen flame, until glowing red hot, and then plunged into a gas jar of oxygen, it glows even brighter and sparkles impressively. (The red-hot iron sometimes falls off the end of the burning spoon on to the base of the gas jar, causing it to crack. This can be avoided by pouring a couple of centimetres of water into the bottom of the gas jar.)

Note: If the solid iron oxide is shaken with water and tested with an indicator, such as litmus, there is no colour change because the oxide is insoluble.

Tin, lead and copper

If heated strongly, tin, lead and copper will burn on the surface to form their oxides (white tin(IV) oxide, yellow lead(II) oxide and black copper(II) oxide).

Practical activity

Metals reacting with water

Potassium, sodium and lithium react vigorously with cold water to produce the hydroxide and to liberate hydrogen gas. Care should be exercised with

(Continued)

(Continued)

these demonstrations because they can explode unpredictably. The safest method of demonstrating these reactions is to use a glass trough, half filled with cold water, and a safety screen above the trough so that any products are kept away from the students (and yourself). Wear goggles or a face shield.

Using tweezers, place the metal on a tile and cut off the required amount (sides no larger than 3 mm) with a scalpel and return the unused metal to its original container. Dry the metal with a tissue to remove the oil before placing it into the trough. Never try to trap the metal as it moves over the surface of the water.

When disposing of apparatus at the end of the demonstration, place all of it in a large bowl of cold water.

Potassium

Potassium reacts vigorously with water and becomes so hot that any hydrogen liberated catches light. Traces of metal in the hydrogen make it burn with a lilac flame. Take care as the potassium usually finishes reacting with a small explosion. The solution left is an alkali (potassium hydroxide) and can be tested with pH paper:

Word equation   Potassium   +   Water $\rightarrow$ Potassium   +   Hydrogen
                                                              hydroxide

Symbol equation $2K\ (s)$ + $2H_2O\ (l)$ $\rightarrow$ $2KOH\ (aq)$ + $H_2\ (g)$

Sodium

Sodium's reaction is slightly less vigorous than potassium and the hydrogen gas usually does not catch light (it can be lit, with care, with a burning splint). If it does catch light, then traces of sodium make it burn with a yellow flame. However, the metal becomes so hot that it melts into a ball as it fizzes over the water's surface. Sodium's reaction is very unpredictable and can explode, ejecting particles of molten metal and the alkali, sodium hydroxide. As before, the remaining solution is alkaline and can be tested with pH paper:

Word equation   Sodium + Water $\rightarrow$ Sodium hydroxide + Hydrogen

Symbol equation $2Na\ (s)$ + $2H_2O\ (l)$ $\rightarrow$ $2NaOH\ (aq)$ + $H_2\ (g)$

Lithium

Lithium's reaction is less vigorous than either potassium or sodium and can safely be demonstrated in a beaker of water rather than a glass trough (a test tube is inadvisable). The lithium fizzes slowly across the surface of the water, releasing hydrogen gas and leaving a solution of the hydroxide. The gas can be collected by inverting an empty test tube over the reacting metal and tested by bring it up to a flame (transfer the tube into an inverted position and place it upright as the flame is approached). As before, the remaining solution can be tested with pH paper:

Word equation   Lithium +   Water   →   Lithium hydroxide + Hydrogen

Symbol equation   2Li (s) + 2H$_2$O (l) →   2LiOH (aq)   +   H$_2$ (g)

Calcium

This reaction is safe for the students to carry out themselves, but with suitable eye protection and ensuring that the metal is not handled directly. Approximately quarter fill a test tube with water and add a small piece of a turning or a small spatula of granules. The metal reacts quite vigorously and the outside of the tube becomes hot to the touch. Hydrogen gas is liberated and can be collected for testing, as above, by placing an upturned tube over the top of the first. The solution formed (calcium hydroxide) is, as before, alkaline, as can be shown with pH paper:

Word equation   Calcium + Water   → Calcium hydroxide + Hydrogen

Symbol equation   2Ca (s) + 2H$_2$O (l) →   2Ca(OH)$_2$ (aq)   +   H$_2$ (g)

Magnesium

In cold water, magnesium is extremely slow to react and takes several days to collect sufficient hydrogen gas to test. A test tube, filled with water, with a short length of magnesium ribbon loosely wedged inside its mouth and inverted in a beaker of water is a suitable method of collecting the gas. The solution formed (magnesium hydroxide) is a very weak alkali, as can be shown with pH paper, and it is used as an antacid:

Word equation   Magnesium + Water   → Magnesium hydroxide + Hydrogen

Symbol equation   2Mg (s)   + 2H$_2$O (l) →   2Mg(OH)$_2$ (aq)   +   H$_2$ (g)

Magnesium burning in steam

Although reacting slowly with cold water, ignited magnesium will continue to burn in steam, forming magnesium oxide and hydrogen. A simple demonstration of this is to ignite a length of magnesium ribbon and to plunge it into the steam coming off a flask of boiling water.

A more effective class practical, however, is to use the apparatus shown in Figure 5.1. This activity involves heating the magnesium in the tube until it

(Continued)

(Continued)

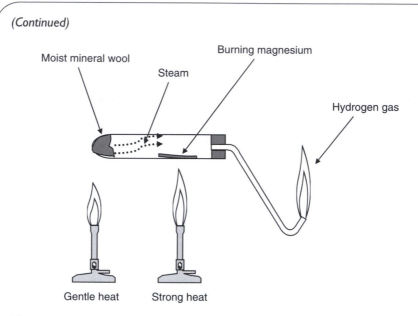

Figure 5.1   Magnesium reacting with steam

ignites and then quickly warming the moist mineral wool so that the steam generated passes over the burning metal. The products are white magnesium oxide and hydrogen. The hydrogen gas evolved can either be ignited as it exits the glass delivery tube or collected in an upturned test tube for testing later:

Word equation   Magnesium + Steam → Magnesium oxide + Hydrogen

Symbol equation $2Mg\ (s)$ $+2H_2O\ (g) →$ $2MgO\ (s)$ $+$ $H_2\ (g)$

Extension activity

As stated above, when magnesium burns in steam it forms white magnesium oxide. However, a dark-grey mark is etched into the side of the test tube. More able students could be set the challenge of explaining this anomaly. (Glass contains silicon compounds and, since magnesium is more reactive than silicon, the compounds are reduced by the magnesium to silicon.)

Iron

Iron will not react with water alone. Iron needs oxygen to be present as well as water in order to rust. The chemical name for rust is hydrated iron(III) oxide. However, in a reaction similar to that above for magnesium, heated iron filings will react with steam to form black diiron(III)iron(II) oxide and hydrogen. This reaction also takes place in iron central-heating radiators, and the 'air lock' commonly referred to is in fact made largely of hydrogen gas. Testing for this gas in a radiator could result in a fire:

Word equation   Iron + Steam $\rightarrow$ Diiron(III)iron(II) oxide + Hydrogen

Symbol equation $3Fe\ (s) + 4H_2O\ (g) \rightarrow$ $Fe_3O_4\ (s)$ $+$ $4H_2\ (g)$

Practical activity

Metals reacting with acids

Due to the reactive natures of potassium, sodium and lithium, it would be very unwise to react them with acids. From calcium on down in the reactivity series, however, the metals can be safely reacted with dilute hydrochloric or sulphuric acid. Nitric acid does not react with most metals in the same way that the other two common acids do – its reactions are more commonly as an oxidizing agent rather than a typical acid, and it would be advisable not to complicate matters by its inclusion.

Acid concentrations of 0.4M or lower will produce a sufficiently vigorous reaction in which the appropriate salt and hydrogen gas are formed. If any heating is required, then it would be safest to place the tube of acid in a bath of hot water because heating directly with a Bunsen could result in boiling acid erupting from the test tube's mouth.

Calcium

With calcium, a single turning or two or three granules of metal added to dilute hydrochloric acid will produce a vigorous, exothermic reaction, liberating hydrogen gas and forming a solution of calcium chloride. With sulphuric acid, the reaction starts but quickly dies down because sparingly soluble calcium sulphate is produced which forms a protective coating around the calcium, preventing further reaction:

Word equation Calcium + Hydrochloric acid $\rightarrow$ Calcium chloride + Hydrogen

Symbol equation $Ca\ (s)\ +$ $2HCl\ (aq)$ $\rightarrow$ $CaCl_2\ (aq)$ $+$ $H_2\ (g)$

Magnesium

It is best to use magnesium ribbon rather than powder or turnings as the reaction is less vigorous and less likely to result in the contents rising out of the tube. With

(Continued)

(Continued)

both acids no heat is needed, and a mildly exothermic reaction results in the production of hydrogen gas and the formation of the respective metal salt solution:

Word equation   Magnesium + Sulphuric acid → Magnesium + Hydrogen
sulphate

Symbol equation $Mg\ (s)$ + $H_2SO_4\ (aq)$ → $MgSO_4\ (aq)$ + $H_2\ (g)$

Iron

Iron filings react very slowly with acids to liberate hydrogen gas and to leave a solution of the respective metal salt. Commercial samples of iron filings often contain impurities of iron(II) sulphide which reacts with acids to release hydrogen sulphide gas that smells of rotten eggs. Students often, mistakenly, interpret this as the smell of hydrogen. As hydrogen sulphide is extremely toxic, even in low concentrations, the students should be deterred from inhaling it. A well ventilated room would be advisable if this reaction were to be carried out as a class practical:

Word equation   Iron + Sulphuric acid → Iron(II) sulphate + Hydrogen

Symbol equation $Fe\ (s)$ + $H_2SO_4\ (aq)$ → $FeSO_4\ (aq)$ + $H_2\ (g)$

Tin and lead

With these two metals, even with heated acid (see above), the reaction with either dilute sulphuric or hydrochloric acid is very slow indeed, and the students are unlikely to observe more than the odd bubble of hydrogen gas being liberated.

Displacement reactions

In general, a metal higher up in the reactivity series will displace a metal lower down in the series from its compounds. This could be in a reaction directly with the other compound or in an aqueous solution. For example, if magnesium metal is added to blue copper(II) sulphate solution, the solution's blue colour fades as it is converted into colourless magnesium sulphate solution and a red/brown precipitate of copper metal collects at the bottom of the container. The more reactive magnesium displaces the less reactive copper from its compound:

Word equation   Magnesium + Copper(II) → Magnesium + Copper
sulphate   sulphate

Symbol equation $Mg\ (s)$ + $CuSO_4\ (aq)$ → $MgSO_4\ (aq)$ + $Cu\ (s)$

Conversely, if iron metal is added to sodium sulphate solution there is no reaction as the iron is lower down in the reactivity series than the sodium. Noting if there is a reaction (or not) when a range of metals is added to a series of compounds will enable the students to construct the reactivity series for themselves.

Note: It is not advisable to use the metals calcium and above in such a series of experiments because they are likely, as outlined above, to react with the solution's water, which would overcomplicate the experiment.

Using a wide range of metals and their compounds in these displacement reactions entails numerous test tubes and racks, considerable volumes of solutions and the opportunity for mistakes. In addition, it can be extremely difficult for a student to observe a reaction if the metal being added and the one being displaced are both silver in colour and if their compounds form colourless solutions. For example, if magnesium metal is added to zinc sulphate solution, an inexperienced observer may record no reaction. As a result, it is wisest to used metals that form coloured compounds. In addition, using spotting tiles for the reactions, as in Figure 5.2, in place of test tubes gives less of an opportunity for mistakes. A limited range of metals and their solutions could include those shown in results Table 5.2. For more able students, using tin metal in place of the lead metal will make the construction of the reactivity series more challenging. More impressive demonstration displacement reactions include the 'silver tree' and thermit(e) reactions.

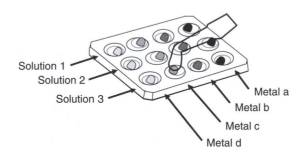

Figure 5.2   Displacement reactions

Table 5.2   *Displacement reactions*

	Magnesium	**Iron**	**Lead**	**Copper**
Magnesium nitrate solution	X			
Iron(II) nitrate solution		X		
Lead(II) nitrate solution			X	
Copper(II) nitrate solution				X

Practical activity

Silver tree

Three quarters fill a boiling tube with silver nitrate solution (expense would prevent this from being a class practical) and stand it in a test-tube rack. Take a 30 cm length of thick copper wire and wrap it round a pencil to form a coil. Remove the copper coil from the pencil and stretch it so that it is slightly longer than the depth of the silver nitrate solution. Place the coil of wire into the silver nitrate solution and leave it to stand overnight. Try not to agitate the solution.

Because copper is higher in the reactivity series than silver, it will displace the silver from its compound and this collects as silver 'leaves' on the copper wire, rather like a silver Christmas tree. The silver nitrate becomes copper(II) nitrate and therefore the solution turns blue/green in colour:

Word equation   Copper + Silver nitrate → Copper(II) nitrate + Copper

Symbol equation $Cu\ (s)\ +\ 2AgNO_3\ (aq) \rightarrow\ Cu(NO_3)_2\ (aq)\ +\ 2Ag\ (s)$

Practical activity

The thermit(e) reaction

This reaction involves aluminium metal displacing iron – aluminium being higher in the reactivity series – from its compound iron(III) oxide, and it is used commercially to weld broken railway lines. For this reaction, the reactants should be perfectly dry and are therefore best stored in a desiccator. Although it is possible to conduct this demonstration in a well ventilated laboratory with small quantities of reactants, a considerable volume of aluminium oxide smoke is generated which, in an open laboratory, may trigger smoke alarms. It would therefore be advisable to check if the alarm system is equipped with a smoke detector or heat sensor. It is not advisable to conduct the reaction in a fume cupboard.

The demonstrator should wear safety spectacles or a face shield, safety screens should be used, and the students should be positioned well away from the reaction and be wearing safety spectacles. Since the reaction produces molten iron and white-hot particles are sometimes ejected, the bench should be protected with heat-proof mats.

The reaction can be performed in a fireclay crucible set in a bucket of sand (see Figure 5.3). Use a mix of 1:3 by weight of aluminium powder to iron(III) oxide. Make a shallow depression in the reaction mixture with a test tube and

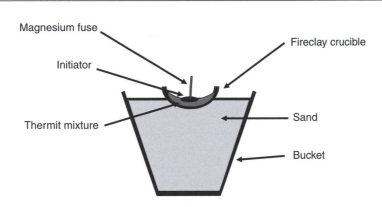

Figure 5.3   Thermit(e) reaction

fill it with an initiator mixture (2 g of barium nitrate carefully mixed with 0.2 g magnesium powder using a wooden or plastic mixing tool). Insert a magnesium ribbon fuse through the initiator mixture so that it extends down well into the reactants. Light the fuse with a Bunsen or small portable blow-torch and stand well back. The reaction is strongly exothermic such that the iron produced is molten:

Word equation   Iron(III) oxide   + Aluminium → Aluminium oxide + Iron

Symbol equation Fe_2O_3 (s)   +   2Al (s)   → Al_2O_3 (s)   + 2Fe (s)

Extraction of metals

It is interesting to compare the reactivity of metals with the date they were first discovered, as in Table 5.3. The more reactive a metal is, the stronger it is bonded to its compounds and the more energy is required to isolate it. Gold, for example, is so unreactive that it does not commonly form compounds and samples of gold metal are found as the solid both underground and on riverbeds. Silver and copper are also sometimes found as the unreacted metal (found native) but when they are found as their compounds they can be obtained by heating the metal oxide with carbon.

This method of extracting metals with carbon can also be used for metals higher in the reactivity series but the higher the metal is in the reactivity series the higher the temperature needed to extract the metal from its ore. Copper, lead and tin, for example, are easily extracted using temperatures obtainable in the laboratory, whereas iron needs a temperature in excess of 1500 °C.

Table 5.3   *Discovery dates of metals*

	Metal	Date first discovered
Most reactive	Potassium	1807
	Sodium	1807
	Calcium	1808
	Magnesium	1808
	Aluminium	1825
	Zinc	1746
	Iron	−2000 BC
	Tin	−3000 BC
	Copper	−3500 BC
	Silver	−5000 BC
Least reactive	Gold	−5000 BC

Practical activity

Extracting metals in the laboratory

Lead

The students should wear safety spectacles and the room should be well ventilated. Mix approximately 1 g of lead(II) oxide in a crucible with 0.1 g of powdered charcoal and a drop of water to moisten the mixture. Cover the mixture with another 0.1 g of charcoal and place the crucible on a pipe-clay triangle on a tripod. Roast the mixture strongly with a roaring Bunsen flame for several minutes. Using a pair of tongs, tip the mixture on to a heatproof mat and small beads of lead metal should be seen. Tipping the heated mixture into a beaker of cold water should allow beads of lead to fall to the bottom while the unreacted carbon floats on the surface.

If the centre of a pencil is made from graphite, why do we call it the 'lead'? Lead metal was once used in pencils but it is a cumulative poison and children, who were in the habit of chewing the ends of their pencils, often suffered from lead poisoning. The lead has been replaced by the safer option of graphite but the name remains.

Tin and copper

Tin and copper can be extracted in the laboratory by the same process outlined above. However, with copper, when the mixture is tipped out on to a heat proof mat, the hot copper appears momentarily pink but will oxidize on the surface to black copper(II) oxide when exposed to the air and this makes it appear that no reaction has taken place. Tipping the hot mixture into a beaker of water should prevent this oxidation.

Iron

Although the temperature needed to extract iron is beyond the capabilities of a Bunsen burner, it is worth unsuccessfully attempting this reaction to stress the need for high temperatures in blast furnaces.

The reactions inside a blast furnace are more complex than simply removing oxygen from iron(III) oxide by heating the oxide with carbon and you would be advised to consult a more detailed text for the precise conditions. In summary, though, the process involves the following stages:

The raw materials – iron ore (iron(III) oxide), coke (carbon) and crushed limestone (calcium carbonate) – are fed into the top of the furnace. These are collectively referred to as the 'charge'. Hot air is fed into the bottom of the furnace.

The carbon first of all burns in the hot air and the heat given off from this exothermic reaction maintains the high temperatures needed for the process:

Word equation   Carbon   +   Oxygen   →   Carbon dioxide

Symbol equation $C\ (s)$ + $O_2\ (g)$ → $CO_2\ (g)$

Carbon is a reducing agent and will remove part of the oxygen from the freshly formed carbon dioxide to produce carbon monoxide:

Word equation   Carbon dioxide   +   Carbon   →   Carbon monoxide

Symbol equation $CO_2\ (g)$ + $C\ (s)$ → $2CO\ (g)$

In turn, the carbon monoxide removes oxygen from the iron(III) oxide and turns back into carbon dioxide, forming iron in the process. At the high temperatures inside the furnace, the iron is a liquid and collects at the base of the furnace:

Word equation Iron(III) oxide + Carbon monoxide → Iron + Carbon dioxide

Symbol equation $Fe_2O_3\ (s)$ + $3CO\ (g)$ → $2Fe\ (s) + 3CO_2\ (g)$

One problem with the extraction process is that the iron formed contains impurities of silicon compounds and carbon, both of which make the iron brittle. The carbon impurities are removed by blowing oxygen gas through molten iron, which turns the carbon to carbon dioxide gas.

There are advantages to removing all the carbon or only part of it. Removing all the carbon produces a very soft malleable iron called wrought iron that is used to make such things as decorative gates. The disadvantage is that the iron is too soft and bendy for other uses. Leaving some carbon in the iron makes it hard but not easy to bend – a juggling act.

The silicon compounds (mainly silicon dioxide – sand) are removed by the limestone which first of all decomposes at the high temperatures to form calcium oxide and gives off carbon dioxide:

(Continued)

(Continued)

Word equation   Calcium carbonate → Calcium oxide + Carbon dioxide

Symbol equation $CaCO_3$ (s)   +   CaO (s)   → CO_2 (g)

The calcium oxide (a basic oxide) then reacts with silicon dioxide (an acidic oxide) in a neutralization reaction to form calcium silicate (slag). The slag produced is also molten and collects at the base of the furnace where it floats on top of the molten iron:

Word equation   Calcium oxide + Silicon dioxide   →   Calcium silicate

Symbol equation   CaO (s)   + SiO_2 (s)   → $CaSiO_3$ (s)

Aluminium

As noted above, the most reactive metals require much higher temperatures to extract than those lower in the reactivity series. Until the early nineteenth century, this method of extracting aluminium was impractical because furnaces capable of sustaining such high temperatures were not generally available, meaning that aluminium was so expensive to extract that it was more costly than gold. Strangely enough, only the most important guests at Court in France were served on aluminium plates, with aluminium cutlery, while the less important had to make do with mere gold!

It is no coincidence that all the most reactive metals were first extracted at around the same time (1807/1808). At this time, methods of generating electricity were devised and this meant that, once electric currents were available, they could be used to extract metals by electrolysis.

In 1886, Charles Hall and Paul Heroult independently proposed similar methods of extracting aluminium from its ore by electrolysis (see Figure 5.4).

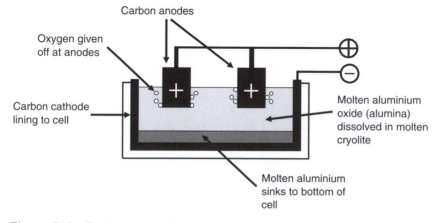

Figure 5.4   Production of aluminium

In summary, using carbon electrodes, a very high direct current is passed through molten aluminium oxide, which separates the aluminium and oxygen. When aluminium oxide is melted, it splits up into aluminium ions and oxygen ions, as in the equation below:

Word equation   Aluminium oxide $\rightarrow$ Aluminium ions   +   Oxygen ions

Symbol equation Al_2O_3 (s) $\rightarrow$ $2Al^{3+}$ (l)   + $3O^{2-}$ (l)

At the cathode

The positive aluminium ions are attracted to the cathode (negative electrode) where they each gain three electrons and become atoms of aluminium which collect at the bottom of the cell as molten aluminium:

Word equation   Aluminium ion   +   Electrons $\rightarrow$ Aluminium atom

Symbol equation Al^{3+} + $3e^-$ $\rightarrow$ Al

At the anode

The negative oxygen ions are attracted to the anode (positive electrode) where they each lose two electrons and become atoms of oxygen. Pairs of oxygen atoms join together to form oxygen molecules, which are released as oxygen gas:

Word equation   Oxygen ion $-$ Electrons $\rightarrow$ Oxygen atom

Symbol equation O^{2-} $-$ $2e^-$ $\rightarrow$ O

Word equation   Oxygen atom   +   Oxygen atom $\rightarrow$ Oxygen molecule

Symbol equation   O   +   O $\rightarrow$ O_2

At the high temperatures inside the furnace, the carbon electrodes burn away in the oxygen produced and have to be constantly replaced.

Aluminium oxide has a very high melting point, which makes it very costly, so a mineral called cryolite (sodium aluminium fluoride) is added to the furnace to allow the aluminium oxide to become liquid at a much lower, and therefore cheaper, temperature.

Practical activity

Metal extraction by electrolysis

The temperatures required to extract aluminium by electrolysis are far too high to be carried out in the laboratory. However, lead(II) bromide has a considerably

(Continued)

(Continued)

lower melting point (373 °C) and can be separated into lead and bromine in the laboratory.

Apparatus

For this activity you will need the following equipment:

- Safety spectacles
- Protective gloves
- Lead(II) bromide (toxic)
- A fume cupboard
- Two small porcelain crucibles
- A 2.5 cm diameter rubber bung with two holes bored through about 1 cm apart
- Two graphite electrodes, about 15 cm long, fitted through the holes in the rubber bung so that about 1cm protrudes above the bung
- A 12 V DC power supply
- Crocodile clips and leads
- A 12 V bulb
- A clamp and stand
- A tripod, pipe-clay triangle, Bunsen burner and heatproof mat

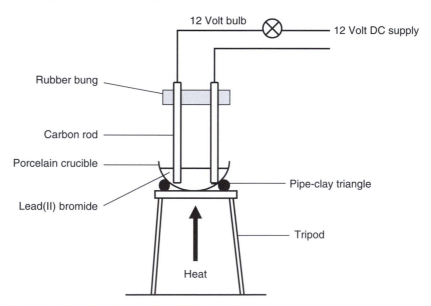

Figure 5.5   Elecrolysis of lead(II) bromide

Method

Arrange the apparatus as shown in Figure 5.5 and demonstrate that, when the lead(II) bromide is solid, no current flows. (Shorting out the carbon rods and the bulb lighting should prove that the bulb lights when the circuit is complete.) Heat the lead(II) bromide in the crucible with a roaring Bunsen flame (this may take a few minutes). When the lead(II) bromide melts, a current will flow (indicated by the bulb lighting up). Molten lead(II) bromide occupies far less space than the solid and therefore the crucible may need topping up with additional powder.

When a current begins to flow, brown fumes of bromine vapour (toxic) can be seen coming from around the anode (+). A white tile held behind the apparatus will help the students to see the bromine. Lead metal is formed around the cathode (−) but cannot seen because it is obscured by the molten lead(II) bromide electrolyte.

Leave the experiment to run for at least 10 minutes then turn off the current. Remove the carbon rods and use tongs to pour the molten lead(II) bromide into a second crucible, leaving a small bead of molten lead behind. Tip the bead of lead on to the heat-proof mat and allow it to cool. Wash any remaining lead(II) bromide from the bead of lead (wearing protective gloves) and the students can test to see that it leaves a mark when dragged across the surface of paper (anyone handling the lead should wash their hands afterwards).

When the lead(II) bromide melts it splits up into lead ions and bromine ions:

Word equation	Lead(II)bromide	$\rightarrow$	Lead ions	+	Bromine ions
Symbol equation	$PbBr_2$ (s)	$\rightarrow$	Pb^{2+} (l)	+	$2Br^-$ (l)

At the cathode

Word equation	Lead ion	+	Electrons	$\rightarrow$	Lead atom
Symbol equation	Pb^{2+}	+	$2e^-$	$\rightarrow$	Pb

At the anode

Word equation	Bromine ion	−	Electron	$\rightarrow$	Bromine atom
Symbol equation	Br^-	−	e^-	$\rightarrow$	Br
Word equation	Bromine atom	+	Bromine atom	$\rightarrow$	Bromine molecule
Symbol equation	Br	+	Br	$\rightarrow$	Br_2

Although lead could be extracted this way, the process is expensive − it is much cheaper to extract it by smelting with carbon.

Electrolysis of potassium iodide

If a similar reaction is carried out using potassium iodide in place of the lead(II) bromide, then purple fumes of iodine are produced at the anode but a lilac flame is seen around the cathode. The reason for the lilac flame is that, although potassium metal is produced, it is extremely reactive and immediately burns in the air to form potassium oxide. Potassium could be produced this way but the process would need to be surrounded by an atmosphere of one of the noble gases.

Currents from simple cells

As can be seen in many of the reactions above, when a metal reacts it gives off electrons and forms a positive ion. For example, when zinc reacts with sulphuric acid, each atom loses two electrons to become a zinc ion, with a double positive charge:

Word equation   Zinc + Sulphuric acid → Zinc sulphate + Hydrogen

Symbol equation Zn (s) + H_2SO_4 (aq)   → $ZnSO_4$ (aq)   + H_2 (g)

What happens   Zn   → Zn^{2+} + $2e^-$
to zinc

The more reactive the metal, the more readily it loses electrons.

If strips of zinc and copper are connected together and placed into sulphuric acid, then the more reactive zinc will give off electrons, while the copper, being far less reactive, will not. Because zinc and copper are both conductors of electricity, some of the electrons will pass from the zinc to the copper, and the second half of the reaction (hydrogen ions from the acid gaining electrons and forming hydrogen gas) will also take place at the copper's surface. Although the copper is not reacting, the hydrogen formed will make it look as though the copper is reacting with the acid. Since there is an additional surface for the second half of the reaction to take place, the zinc wears away much faster than it would on its own.

If, instead of connecting the metals directly, they are connected via a wire, electrons will flow from the zinc through the wire to the copper. You now have a simple cell. This process will work with any two different metals connected this way and placed in a solution with which one metal will react. The bigger the difference in reactivity between the two metals, the greater the voltage (but the faster the more reactive metal will be used up). The more reactive metal reacts much faster than it would alone, while the less reactive metal reacts more slowly than it would alone. This process can not only cause problems but it can also be put to use.

Problems

With a traditional tin can, the can is made from steel (mainly iron) with a tin coating. Interestingly, the tin usually protects the steel from the contents of the can, rather than the atmosphere. If the tin coating is scratched, you are in the position of having a reactive metal (iron) in contact with the less reactive metal (tin) in the presence of either a slightly acidic atmosphere or, perhaps, if the can contains fruit, acidic contents. In this case, the iron reacts faster than it would on its own and the protective coating hastens its demise.

Uses

Underground water pipes, canal barges and ships are all constructed from iron, which will rust rapidly in their environment. It would be impractical to remove an ocean-going liner from the water in order to paint the underside. A more practical option is to bolt blocks of magnesium metal to the underside of the structure. Once again, a simple cell is produced in which the more reactive magnesium reacts faster than it would alone, while the iron structure reacts more slowly than it would otherwise do. Periodically, the corroded blocks of magnesium are replaced with fresh ones. The process is called sacrificial protection.

Engaging activity

Emergency power supply for a calculator

Apparatus

For this activity you will need the following equipment:

- Leads, crocodile clips and voltmeter
- A 250 cm³ beaker
- A small battery-operated calculator
- A small torch
- An iron nail
- Copper foil or thick wire
- Lead foil
- Aluminium foil
- Zinc foil
- Table salt
- A lemon or any other citrus fruit
- Vinegar
- A potato
- Water

Method

Having established above that a simple cell can be produced using an electrolyte and two different metals, the students are set the challenge to produce a simple cell from everyday materials that will have a sufficiently high voltage to run a small calculator.

(Continued)

(Continued)

As an extension activity, the students could be set the challenge of producing a cell (or combination of cells) that would power a small torch.

Engaging activity

Turning base metal into gold

This is a novel demonstration in which a copper coin appears to be turned first of all into silver and then into gold.

Apparatus

For this activity you will need the following equipment:

- Safety spectacles
- Protective gloves
- A Bunsen burner
- A 250 cm^3 beaker
- A tripod, gauze and protective mat
- Metal tongs
- A stirring rod
- Zinc powder
- Steel wool
- A copper 2p piece
- 100 cm^3 of 1 M sodium hydroxide solution (corrosive)

Method

Clean the surface of the coin with the steel wool and place it to one side.

Place approximately 100 cm^3 of 1 M sodium hydroxide solution into the beaker and heat it on the tripod and gauze until it almost reaches boiling point. Turn the Bunsen off. Slowly add four or five heaped spatulas of zinc powder to the hot sodium hydroxide solution. Some of the zinc will dissolve in the solution and hydrogen gas will be given off. Any unreacted zinc will form a layer at the bottom of the beaker.

Place the copper coin into the sodium hydroxide solution so that it is in contact with the unreacted zinc. Leave the coin in the solution for no longer than 2–3 minutes when it should gain a shiny silver coating.

Remove the coin from the beaker with tongs and thoroughly wash it under the tap to remove any impurities. The coin is now safe to pass among the class.

Using tongs, heat both sides of the shiny silver coin over a roaring Bunsen flame for a few seconds and a shiny gold surface should be formed. Allow the coin to cool when it should be safe to pass around the class.

Explanation

Some of the zinc metal reacts with the sodium hydroxide solution to form a solution of sodium zincate and hydrogen gas:

Word equation Zinc + Sodium hydroxide + Water → Sodium zincate + Hydrogen

Symbol equation $Zn\ (s) + 2NaOH\ (aq) + 2H_2O\ (l) \rightarrow Na_2[Zn(OH)_4]\ (aq) + H_2\ (aq)$

Some of the zinc atoms give off electrons and become zinc ions:

Word equation Zinc metal → Zinc ions + Electrons

Ionic equation $Zn \rightarrow Zn^{2+} + 2e^-$

The zinc ions then react with the sodium hydroxide solution to form the complex zincate ion, $[Zn(OH)_4]^{2-}$ (aq)

At the surface of the copper, these complex ions gain electrons (flowing from the zinc) and zinc metal is formed:

Word equation Zincate ion + Electrons → Zinc + Hydroxide ions

Ionic equation $[Zn(OH)_4]^{2-}\ (aq) + 2e^- \rightarrow Zn\ (s) + 4OH^-\ (aq)$

The shiny zinc makes it look as though the coin has been turned into silver.

When the coin is heated in the roaring Bunsen flame, the zinc coating and the copper beneath combine to form the alloy brass.

Further reading

Hutchings, K. (2000) *Classic Chemistry Experiments.* Cambridge: Royal Society of Chemistry.
  A comprehensive guide to a whole range of chemistry demonstrations.

Jones, A., Clemmet, M., Higton, A. and Golding, E. (1999) *Access to Chemistry.* Cambridge: Royal Society of Chemistry.
  A good study guide that prepares the reader for A-level chemistry courses or those of an equivalent standing.

Ryan, L. (2006) *New Chemistry for You.* Cheltenham: Nelson Thornes.
  A general chemistry text that covers a broad spectrum of GCSE chemistry topics.

Shakhashiri, B. Z. (1992) *Chemical Demonstrations 4: A Handbook for Teachers of Chemistry.* Madison, WI: University of Winsconsin Press.
  Contains a range of impressive reactivity series and electrochemistry demonstrations.

6 Acids and bases
Mark Crowley and John Twidle

This chapter covers:

- using indicators to test for acidity
- the importance of water in the properties of acids
- the pH scale and its meaning
- the difference between strong and concentrated acids
- neutralization and characteristic acid reactions
- acids and alkalis in the environment.

Test your own knowledge

Before reading the material in this chapter test your current knowledge with the following questions:

1. Which common acids do you know? What common alkalis can you name?
2. What is the difference between a base and an alkali?
3. What colour is litmus indicator when add to a) alkali; b) acid; c) water?
4. What do the following values on the pH scale indicate: pH 1, 4, 7, 10 and 14?
5. If a substance is added to acid and it fizzes, the gas evolved can be collected. How would you test for a) CO_2; b) O_2; c) H_2?

Acids and alkalis

The word 'acid' comes from the Latin word *acidus*, meaning sour, and 'alkali' from the Arabic *al-kali*, meaning burnt to ashes, as the first alkalis to be used were the remains of burnt plant material. Many people hold the common idea of acids being dangerous, corrosive liquids. However, acids can be obtained as solids, liquids and gases (for example, citric acid, which is present in a variety of fruits and vegetables, exists as a white crystalline powder at room temperature).

Vinegar (or ethanoic acid) gets its name from *vinum acre*, the Latin for sour wine. Ascorbic acid (or vitamin c) gets its name from the Latin *ascorbutus*, meaning no scurvy, because it was used to prevent sailors suffering from scurvy during long sea voyages.

Students (and some teachers) often confuse the terms 'alkali' and 'base'. A base is any metal oxide or hydroxide. If the oxide or hydroxide is soluble in water, then the solution is called an alkali. So all alkalis are bases but not all bases are alkalis.

Engaging activity

Water into wine

Apparatus

For this activity you will need the following equipment:

- Three 250 cm³ beakers
- Phenolphthalein indicator
- 1 M sodium hydroxide solution
- 1 M hydrochloric acid

Method

In advance, rinse out the first beaker with sodium hydroxide solution and pour the alkali solution away, leaving a trace in the beaker. Also in advance, rinse out the second beaker with the hydrochloric acid and pour the acid solution away, leaving a trace behind.

Beakers 1 and 2 are contaminated with alkali and acid but appear to be empty. Add 150 cm³ water to the third beaker and a little phenolphthalein indicator. The solution should remain colourless.

When the indicator solution is poured into beaker 1 it will change colour to a pink/purple (red wine). When the mixture is poured into beaker 2 it will lose its colour again (it will turn back into water).

Note: Be careful not to allow the students to drink any of the liquids. Apart from the corrosive nature of the acids and alkalis, phenolphthalein has laxative properties.

(Continued)

(Continued)

Hydrogen chloride, HCl (g), exists as a gas a room temperature. In each molecule of hydrogen chloride, hydrogen and chlorine atoms are joined by a single covalent bond. If cooled to −85.1°C, hydrogen chloride forms a colourless liquid which, if kept dry, is not considered an acid.

The acidic behaviour of hydrogen chloride is only exhibited when it mixes with water. In a humid atmosphere fumes of hydrochloric acid are formed at the neck of a bottle of hydrogen chloride.

Hydrochloric acid is an aqueous solution of hydrogen chloride, HCl (aq). In water the neutral covalent molecules of hydrogen chloride undergo an important change to form charged ions.

Practical activity

The importance of water

Apparatus

For this activity you will need the following equipment:

- Four test tubes
- Citric acid crystals
- Distilled water
- Magnesium ribbon

Method

Number the test tubes from 1 to 4. Add the following combinations of materials to each test tube:

- *Test tube 1*: a spatula of citric acid.
- *Test tube 2*: a strip of magnesium.
- *Test tube 3*: a spatula of citric acid and a strip of magnesium.
- *Test tube 4*: a spatula of citric acid and a strip of magnesium.

Finally, add 5 cm³ distilled water into all the test tubes except 4.

You should clearly see fizzing in only the tube with citric acid, magnesium *and* water. Test tube 2 may begin to form bubbles but not as vigorously as the acidified solution. Magnesium reacts slowly with water.

More than aqueous solutions

Whenever an acidic compound is added to water, its molecules break up (*dissociate*) to release positive hydrogen ions, H^+, and negative ions. The other ions which acids release are important in forming salts.

The general equation used to show the dissociation of an acid (HA) is:

$$HA \text{ (state)} + H_2O(l) \rightarrow H^+ \text{ (aq)} + A^- \text{ (aq)}$$

The production of hydrogen ions by acids, when they dissolve in water, is a reversible reaction. This means that molecules are constantly breaking apart (dissociating) and ions are recombining to form neutral molecules. These opposing processes find a natural balance which might favour the dissociated ions or undissociated molecule.

Several acids, such as sulphuric acid, can release more than one hydrogen ion per molecule. Sulphuric acid can dissociate in two stages to release two H^+ ions:

$$H_2SO_4 \text{ (aq)} \rightarrow H^+ \text{ (aq)} + HSO_4^- \text{ (aq)}$$

$$HSO_4^- \text{ (aq)} \rightarrow H^+ \text{ (aq)} + SO_4^{2-} \text{ (aq)}$$

Alkalis such as sodium hydroxide and calcium hydroxide, dissolve in water to give *hydroxide* ions (OH^-):

$$NaOH \text{ (s)} + H_2O \text{ (l)} \rightarrow Na^+ \text{ (aq)} + OH^- \text{ (aq)}$$

$$Ca(OH)_2 \text{ (s)} + H_2O \text{ (l)} \rightarrow Ca^{2+} \text{ (aq)} + 2OH^- \text{ (aq)}$$

Revising pH

Acids and alkalis are considered to be chemical opposites. A simple test to tell the difference between acids and alkalis is to use an indicator, such as litmus, which turns red in an acid and blue in an alkali.

Litmus is an indicator that has been known for hundreds of years. It is a mixture of different water-soluble dyes. These naturally occurring dyes are extracted from lichens which grow in warm climates. Other natural indicators can be obtained from cherries, elderberries, red cabbage and blackberries. Beetroot is also commonly used to produce a natural indicator but can be rather messy. A less messy option is to use beetroot crisps rather than the raw vegetable.

Although indicators can test to see if a chemical is an acid or alkali, they do not necessarily tell how strong the acid or alkali solution is. A better test for the strength of an acid is to measure its pH.

When we measure the pH of an acid, we are measuring the amount of the positively charged hydrogen ions in the solution. The pH scale is not a simple linear scale – it is logarithmic. Each unit increase in pH ($1 \rightarrow 2$, $2 \rightarrow 3$, $3 \rightarrow 4$...) represents a drop in the concentration of H^+ ions by a factor of ten:

pH	1	2	3	4	5	6
[H^+]	$0{\cdot}1(10^{-1})$	$0{\cdot}01(10^{-2})$	$0{\cdot}001(10^{-3})$	$0{\cdot}0001(10^{-4})$	$0{\cdot}00001(10^{-5})$	$0{\cdot}000001(10^{-6})$

[H^+] = hydrogen ion concentration in mol dm^{-3}.

More on pH

The pH scale was developed by Dr Søren Sørensen, head of Carlsberg Laboratory's Chemical Department in 1909. He developed the pH scale during his research into the action of enzymes on proteins. Sørensen determined the hydrogen ion concentration involved in his experiments through conductivity experiments. He converted the concentrations into his pH scale to represent 'the power of hydrogen':

$$pH = -\log_{10}[H^+] \text{ and } [H^+] = 10^{-pH}$$

Note: This calculation is probably well beyond the understanding of all but the most able students.

Practical activity

Investigating the relative strengths of the pH scale

Apparatus

For this activity you will need the following equipment:

- A 10 cm^3 measuring cylinder
- Distilled water
- 0.1 M hydrochloric acid
- Universal indicator
- A pH indicator chart
- A spotting tile
- A pipette – clean thoroughly between each sample

Note: It is possible to use a pH meter to measure the strength of an acidic or alkaline solution but a simpler and cheaper option is to use universal indicator, which is a combination of indicators that change colour at each pH.

Method

Start with 10 cm³ 0.1 M hydrochloric acid in the measuring cylinder. Using a pipette, transfer a few drops to a dimple on the spotting tile. Pour away all but 1 cm³ of the original acid. Dilute the remaining acid with 9 cm³ distilled water. Transfer a few drops of this solution to the next dimple on the spotting tile.

Carefully pour away all but 1 cm³ of the diluted acid. Dilute the remaining acid with 9 cm³ distilled water. Transfer a few drops of this solution to the next dimple on the spotting tile.

Repeat the dilutions four more times, each time transferring a few drops of the solution to the next dimple on the spotting tile. Finally, add universal indicator to each collected (diluted) sample and observe the colours obtained.

As an extension, the students could be asked to repeat the experiment starting with 0.1 M sodium hydroxide solution.

Commonly the pH scale runs from 1 to 14. Theoretically, however, the pH of some solutions can extend either side of these values. Solutions with a pH less than 7 are acidic, and solutions with a pH greater than 7 are basic or alkaline.

Practical activity

Demonstrating universal indicator's range of colours

Apparatus

For this activity you will need the following equipment:

- A glass tube 60 cm long and about 1 cm in diameter
- A stand and clamp
- Two rubber bungs to fit the glass tube
- A 250 cm³ beaker
- Two dropping pipettes
- Universal indicator solution
- 0.1 M hydrochloric acid
- 0.1 M sodium hydroxide solution
- Distilled water

(Continued)

(Continued)

Method

Add sufficient universal indicator to about 100 cm³ distilled water in the beaker to give a strong green solution. Place one of the bungs firmly into the bottom end of the tube and hold the tube vertically in a stand with the clamp. Pour the green universal indicator solution into the tube so that it is 1 or 2 cm from the top. It is important that a small air gap is left at the top of the tube when both bungs are in place.

Add five or six drops of the sodium hydroxide solution to the top of the tube and stopper that end as well. Remove the tube from the clamp, invert it and replace the tube in the clamp. Remove the top bung and add five drops of hydrochloric acid to the tube. Replace the bung.

Remove the tube from the clamp and slowly invert the tube three or four times so that the rising air bubble mixes the tube's contents. You should have the full spectrum of universal indicator colours in the tube, from red to purple.

Classifying acids and bases

Types of acid

Care should be taken when referring to an acid as being strong or concentrated and weak or dilute. The terms 'dilute' and 'concentrated' indicate how much acid has been dissolved in a solvent, usually water.

An acid's concentration is based on the number of moles of solute and the volume of solvent used:

$$\text{Concentration} = \frac{\text{Amount of substance}}{\text{Volume}} = \frac{\text{mol}}{\text{dm}^3}$$

Acid of 1 M contains one mole of acid dissolved in 1000 cm³ of water. (1 M = 1 mol dm⁻³). Typically, students will use volumes of around 25 cm³ (0.025 dm³) and concentrations close to 0.1 M. For this volume and concentration:

$$\text{Concentration} = 0.1 \text{ M} = \frac{0.0025 \text{ mol}}{0.025 \text{ dm}^3}$$

0.0025 mol of nitric acid, HNO_3 = 0.158 g

The concentration of an acid can be increased by dissolving more acid, or decreased by adding more water. The strength of an acid refers to the amount of dissociation which occurs in water. Some acids dissociate more easily than others.

Hydrochloric acid is formed when hydrogen chloride gas dissolves in water – up to 72 g of the gas dissolves in 100 cm^3 of water at room temperature. Hydrochloric acid is a strong acid. It is an acid that, in effect, dissociates completely in an aqueous solution. First:

$$HCl\ (g) + H_2O\ (l) \rightarrow HCl\ (aq)$$

Then:

$$HCl\ (aq)\ \rightarrow H^+\ (aq) + Cl^-\ (aq)$$

Note the two stages involved: first the gas dissolves to form an aqueous solution (aq), then the dissolved molecules split to form ions.

Ethanoic acid is a liquid a room temperature which readily mixes with water. Ethanoic acid is a typical weak acid. It reacts with water to produce hydrogen ions and ethanoate ions. However the reverse reaction also takes place, and the ions very easily recombine to form the neutral acid molecule. First:

$$CH_3CO_2H\ (l) + H_2O\ (l) \rightarrow\ CH_3CO_2H\ (aq)$$

Then:

$$CH_3CO_2H\ (aq)\ \rightarrow H^+\ (aq) + CH_3CO_2^-\ (aq)$$
$$\text{Ethanoic acid} \qquad\qquad \text{Ethanoate ions}$$

Pure water is neither acid nor alkaline. The pH for pure water at 25 °C is 7.0. Water itself can dissociate:

$$H_2O\ (l)\ \rightarrow H^+\ (aq) + OH^-\ (aq)$$

As it dissociates, it forms equal amounts of H^+ and OH^- ions. Hence water is considered neutral.

Just as acids can be defined as strong or weak, so can alkalis.

Irritant vs. corrosive

The word 'corrosion' is derived from the Latin verb *corrodere*, which means 'to gnaw'. A corrosive substance is one that causes destruction or irreversible damage to living tissue on contact with it. Corrosive substances include strong acids, strong bases and concentrated solutions of certain weak acids and weak bases. When in contact with living tissue, many corrosive materials catalyse the hydrolysis of esters, amides and proteins.

A low concentration of a corrosive substance is usually an irritant. Irritants are considered to be chemicals that cause a reversible inflammatory effect on living tissue. Inflammation can occur on immediate, prolonged or repeated contact with an irritant.

In cases where research scientists are working with novel materials and with no known safety data, if the pH of the material is <2 or >11.5, the substances are assumed to be corrosive.

Creating salts

The term 'salt' can be a source of confusion for some students. Common table salt (or sodium chloride) is just one example of a chemical salt; many more salts exist. In chemistry, a salt is the substance formed when either all or part of an acid's hydrogen is replaced by a metal.

To produce a salt such as lithium nitrate ($LiNO_3$), the hydrogen in nitric acid (HNO_3) is replaced by lithium ions. Salts are ionic compounds. They contain cations (positively charged ions) and anions (negative ions). The name of a salt starts with the name of the cation (e.g. lithium) followed by the name of the anion. (e.g. nitrate).

Neutralization

Neutralization is a chemical reaction in which an acid and a base, or alkali, react to produce salt and water. For an alkali, we can write the general equation:

$$Acid + Alkali \rightarrow Salt + Water$$

For example:

$$HCl\ (aq) + NaOH\ (aq) \rightarrow NaCl\ (aq) + H_2O\ (1)$$

Since hydrochloric acid is a strong acid and sodium hydroxide a strong base, we can rewrite this reaction in terms of the ions involved:

$$H^+Cl^-\ (aq) + Na^+OH^-\ (aq) \rightarrow Na^+Cl^-\ (aq) + H_2O\ (1)$$

Study the change occurring in the reaction above carefully – both sodium ions (Na^+) and chloride ions (Cl^-) remain dissociated, ignoring these 'spectator' ions, the most important change becomes:

$$H^+ (aq) + OH^- (aq) \rightarrow H_2O (l)$$

Neutralization converts hydrogen cations and hydroxide anions into neutral molecules of water. When we bring together equal numbers of H^+ cations and OH^- anions, the resulting solution has a pH of 7.0. It is neutral.

Practical activity

Neutralization experiments

Standard titration

When adding strong acids to strong alkalis to form a neutral solution, the precise point of neutralization can be difficult to attain. The pH rapidly changes at the point of neutralization and is easily overshot. In this activity neutralization is demonstrated by the slow addition of one solution (a mixture of strong and weak acids) to a second (a similar mixture of alkalis).

Apparatus

For this activity you will need the following equipment:

- A burette (50 cm³)
- A stand and clamp
- Two 100 cm³ beakers
- Universal indicator solution
- 0.1M hydrochloric acid
- 1M ethanoic acid
- 0.1M sodium hydroxide solution
- 1M ammonia solution (ammonium hydroxide)

Method

Place 10 cm³ sodium hydroxide into a beaker and add 10 cm³ ammonia solution. Add several drops of universal indicator. Measure out 40 cm³ hydrochloric acid

(Continued)

(Continued)

into the second beaker and add 40 cm³ ethanoic acid solution. Add several drops of universal indicator.

Carefully fill the burette with the acid mix – ensure that the tap/jet is filled with the acid solution. Fix the burette in a stand so that it is above the beaker of alkalis.

Run the acid into the conical flask 1 cm³ at a time, stirring between each addition. The indicator colour may fade – be prepared to add more drops of solution. Continue adding acid until a pH of 7 is reached – the point of neutralization. Open the tap and allow the acid to drain into the beaker. The pH will fall down to 1.

Thermometric/conductimetric titration

Neutralization is an exothermic process – there is a net release of energy. As acid is added to alkali its temperature rises. Once the alkali has been neutralized, any further addition of acid remains unreacted – the addition of the excess acid, at room temperature, to the warm neutral mixture lowers the temperature.

Solutions of acids and alkalis contain free ions and behave as electrically conductive materials – they are electrolytes. Adding an acid to an alkali causes hydrogen and hydroxide ions to form neutral water.

In forming a neutral mixture, the conductivity of a reaction mixture drops. *Note:* It does not fall to zero because the reaction mixture contains ionic salts. By studying the temperature and conductivity of a reaction mixture, the point of neutralization can be determined without indicators.

Apparatus

For this activity you will need the following equipment:

- A burette (50 cm³)
- A stand and clamp
- A 100 cm³ beaker
- 1 M hydrochloric acid
- 1 M sodium hydroxide solution
- A temperature probe/thermometer
- Graphite rods
- An ammeter
- A 4.5 V battery/DC supply
- Crocodile clips and connecting wires

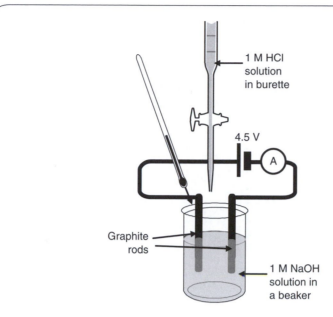

1 M HCl
solution
in burette

4.5 V

A

Graphite
rods

1 M NaOH
solution in
a beaker

Figure 6.1   Conductimetric titration

Method

Place 20 cm³ of sodium hydroxide into the beaker. Carefully fill the burette with the acid, ensuring that the tap/jet is filled with acid. Fix the burette in a stand so that it is above the beaker of alkali. Put the two electrodes into the beaker vertically and connect them to the voltage supply, in series with the ammeter. Add the thermometer/probe to the beaker (see Figure 6.1).

Run the acid into the conical flask 1 cm³ at a time, stirring between each addition. This can be difficult with the probes and electrodes. If possible the whole apparatus could be set up over a magnetic stirrer. Record the temperature and current after each addition. Continue adding acid until a total of 20 cm³ has been added to the alkali.

Note: Using 4.5 V helps generate a high current (0.4 A) but causes electrolysis of the solution. This will generate small quantities of poisonous chlorine gas. Remove the battery as soon as the titration is complete.

Plotting the results of this experiment typically yields the chart shown in Figure 6.2. Temperature reaches a maximum as current reaches a minimum. This occurs at the point of neutralization.

The students could carry out a simplified version of thermometric titration by combining a fixed volume of acid with varying volumes of alkali (see Figure 6.3).

(Continued)

(Continued)

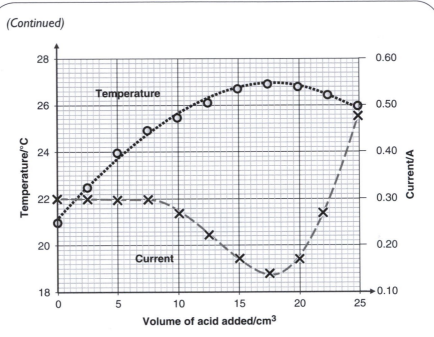

Figure 6.2   Conductimetric and thermometric titration curves

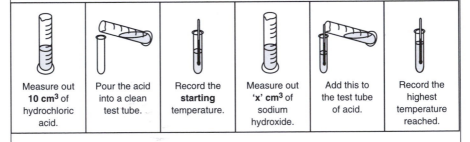

| Measure out **10 cm³** of hydrochloric acid. | Pour the acid into a clean test tube. | Record the **starting** temperature. | Measure out **'x' cm³** of sodium hydroxide. | Add this to the test tube of acid. | Record the highest temperature reached. |

Figure 6.3   Student version of thermometric titration

Different groups within a class could be asked to add a particular volume of sodium hydroxide (2, 4, 6, 8 cm³...). Each group's results can then be combined to determine what volume of sodium hydroxide was needed to reach the point of neutralization. *Note:* Do not encourage the students to stir with the thermometer.

Acid drops and bicarbonate

Warning! This experiment is at odds with the laboratory rules we usually enforce, namely – no eating in class. The students should be advised to wash their hands first and to keep the foodstuff away from other equipment – it is best if the tables are completely clear.

Apparatus

For this activity you will need the following equipment:

- Crushed acid drops (use a kitchen mortar and pestle)
- Baking powder
- Teaspoons rather than spatulas
- Sterile petri dishes or clean paper towels

Method

Measure out a small amount of the crushed acid drops on to each dish/paper towel. On a separate dish/paper towel, place a heaped teaspoon of baking powder.

Ask the students to stick out their tongues and to keep these out. Next, tell them to place a piece of crushed acid drop on to their tongues – if they swallow it, the experiment will not work.

Now ask them to take a pinch of baking soda and slowly to sprinkle the powder on top of the acid drop. They should add enough so that the sour taste of the acid drops is neutralized.

Acid + metal

Salts are formed when the hydrogen in an acid is replaced by metals or metallic radicals. Salts can be formed by directly combining reactive metals with acids:

$$\text{Acid} + \text{Metal} \rightarrow \text{Salt} + \text{Hydrogen}$$

For example:

$$2HCl \text{ (aq)} + Mg \text{ (s)} \rightarrow MgCl_2 \text{ (aq)} + H_2 \text{ (g)}$$

This salt-forming reaction is also considered to be a displacement reaction – the magnesium displaces the hydrogen. Metals such as gold, silver and copper are not sufficiently reactive to displace hydrogen from dilute acids.

Usually acids and metals behave in a predictable way: the more reactive the metal and the more concentrated the acid, the faster the production of hydrogen gas. However, nitric acid and some concentrated acids do not behave as predicted.

Nitric acid is an oxidizing agent and hydrogen (H_2) is rarely formed when it reacts with a metal. Only magnesium (Mg), manganese (Mn) and calcium (Ca) react with cold, dilute nitric acid to give hydrogen. If you intend to generate and test hydrogen, the best acid to use is hydrochloric acid.

Practical activity

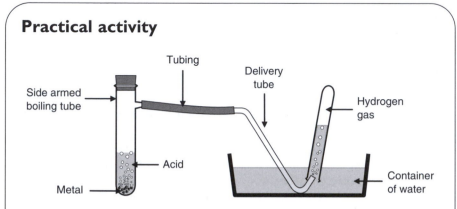

Figure 6.4   Collecting hydrogen over water

Collecting hydrogen gas

The apparatus shown in Figure 6.4 is typically used for preparing and collecting hydrogen. This method allows the students to collect several tubes of gas. These can then be used to test for the presence of hydrogen with lighted splints. Ensure the students handle this apparatus carefully – they should try not to spill the water or break the delivery tubes.

Note: Ignore the first tube or two of gas collected – this will be mainly air pushed through the equipment as hydrogen is evolved. Collect a quarter to a third of a tube of hydrogen gas. Lift the tube out of the water and allow the air to replace the water. Stopper the tube and allow the air (oxygen) and hydrogen to mix. A loud pop will be heard when this mixture is tested with a lighted splint.

If time is tight or you do not have sufficient equipment, a second, much quicker method is as follows.

Apparatus

For this activity you will need the following equipment:

- Two test tubes
- A reactive metal, such as magnesium (3 cm)
- 0.5 M hydrochloric acid
- A small measuring cylinder
- A naked flame (Bunsen or lighted candle)
- A wood splint

Method

Measure out 10 cm³ of acid into one of the test tubes. Add the magnesium ribbon and quickly invert the empty test tube on top (see Figure 6.5). The students need to keep the two tubes held firmly together for at least one minute.

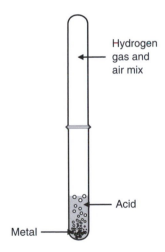

Hydrogen
gas and
air mix

Acid

Metal

Figure 6.5   A quick method for collecting hydrogen

Pull the top tube away and quickly cover the open end with a thumb (or rubber bung). Have a lighted split ready. Uncover the tube and insert the lighted splint a short way into the tube. There should be a loud pop. If this does not work, then the hydrogen in the test tube above the reaction mixture can be tested in the same way.

Acid + base

Salts are formed when an acid is neutralized by a base. Most bases are solid metal oxides. A number of bases are water soluble but the majority are insoluble. The general equation is:

$$\text{Acid} + \text{Base} \rightarrow \text{Salt} + \text{Water}$$

For example:

$$2\text{HCl (aq)} + \text{MgO (s)} \rightarrow \text{MgCl}_2 \text{ (aq)} + \text{H}_2\text{O (l)}$$

A common approach when neutralizing an acid is to add an excess of the solid base to the acid. Any base which the remains after the acid has been used up can be filtered off. The subsequent solution contains just chemical salt and water.

The careful evaporation of the water from the reaction mixture causes crystallization to take place. Many salts are able to form crystals which incorporate water molecules in their crystal structure. Blue copper sulphate crystals contain a great deal of this trapped water. Its crystals are hydrated and are given the formula, $CuSO_4.5H_2O$ – the '.' indicates 'water of crystallization'.

Practical activity

Copper oxide to copper sulphate crystals

Apparatus

For this activity you will need the following equipment:

- A 50 cm³ beaker
- A Bunsen burner, tripod, heat-proof mat and gauze
- A filter funnel and filter paper
- An evaporating basin
- A spatula
- 1 M sulphuric acid (20 cm³)
- Copper oxide (2–3 g)

Method

The method for producing copper sulphate crystals in this way is shown in Figure 6.6.

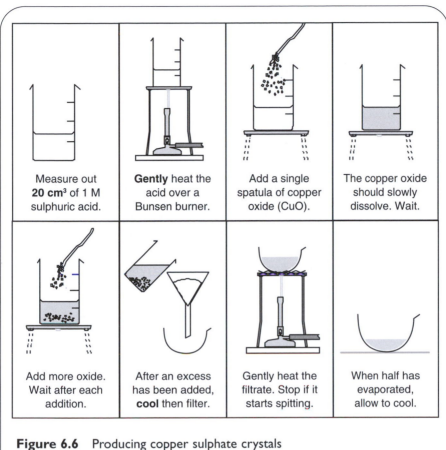

Measure out **20 cm³** of 1 M sulphuric acid.	**Gently** heat the acid over a Bunsen burner.	Add a single spatula of copper oxide (CuO).	The copper oxide should slowly dissolve. Wait.
Add more oxide. Wait after each addition.	After an excess has been added, **cool** then filter.	Gently heat the filtrate. Stop if it starts spitting.	When half has evaporated, allow to cool.

Figure 6.6   Producing copper sulphate crystals

Acid + carbonate

When acids and metals react, they effervesce (fizz), producing hydrogen gas. Effervescence is the escape of gas from an aqueous solution. Acids also effervesce with carbonates but the gas produced is carbon dioxide. Salts are also formed at the same time:

$$\text{Acid} + \text{Carbonate} \rightarrow \text{Salt} + \text{Water} + \text{Carbon dioxide}$$

For example:

Sulphuric acid		*Copper carbonate*		*Copper sulphate*		*Water*		*Carbon dioxide*
H_2SO_4 (aq)	+	$CuCO_3$ (s)	$\rightarrow$	$CuSO_4$ (aq)	+	H_2O (l)	+	CO_2 (g)

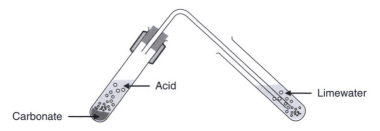

Figure 6.7   Collecting and testing carbon dioxide

The presence of carbon dioxide can be tested by passing the gas produced into a saturated solution of calcium hydroxide (limewater) (see Figure 6.7). Carbon dioxide reacts with calcium hydroxide to form a white precipitate of calcium carbonate. We commonly say that the limewater turns cloudy:

Limewater		*Carbon dioxide*		*Calcium carbonate*		*Water*
$Ca(OH)_2$ (aq)	+	CO_2 (g)	$\rightarrow$	$CaCO_3$ (s)	+	H_2O (l)

An interesting practical based on acid effervescence with carbonate is the rainbow fizz experiment.

Engaging activity

The rainbow fizz

This experiment combines acids, indicators, salts, effervescence and neutralization in one! It can be used as an interesting summary or to provoke interest at the start of the topic.

Apparatus

For this activity you will need the following equipment:

- A test-tube rack
- A boiling tube containing about 2 g anhydrous sodium carbonate
- A 10 cm³ measuring cylinder
- Universal indicator solution
- Two test tubes, each containing about 5 cm³ dilute ethanoic acid (4% ethanoic acid in water)

Method

Measure out 5 cm³ water with the measuring cylinder and add it to the anhydrous sodium carbonate. Gently shake the tube so that the sodium carbonate dissolves. Feel the outside of the tube (what does this tell you about the process of dissolving sodium carbonate in water?).

Add about 10 drops of universal indicator to the solution and note the colour (what does this tell you about sodium carbonate solution?). Add one of the tubes of ethanoic acid to the solution (do not shake the tube) and note what happens. Add the second tube of acid to the mixture (do not shake the tube) and note any further changes.

Acids and alkalis in the environment

Acids around us

Traces of carbon dioxide naturally found in the atmosphere dissolve in rainwater to form carbonic acid. Carbonic acid splits up in water into hydrogen ions, hydrogencarbonate (bicarbonate) ions and a few carbonate ions:

$$CO_2 \text{ (g)} + H_2O \text{ (l)} \rightarrow H_2CO_3 \text{ (aq)}$$

Then:

$$H_2CO_3 \text{ (aq)} \rightarrow H^+ \text{ (aq)} + HCO_3^- \text{ (aq)}$$

And to a lesser extent:

$$HCO_3^- \text{ (aq)} \rightarrow H^+ \text{ (aq)} + CO_3^{2-} \text{ (aq)}$$

For carbonic acid, there are far more original undissociated acid molecules in solution than dissociated ions. It is therefore a weak acid. This means that rainwater is naturally slightly acidic.

Unlike solids, gases tend to be less soluble in hot water than in cold. Heating a solution of carbonic acid causes dissolved carbon dioxide to form bubbles and escape from the solution. The reactions shown above start to reverse. This removes H^+ from the solution and causes the rise in pH, so the solution becomes less acidic.

Practical activity

Carbonic acid and gas solubility

Apparatus

For this activity you will need the following equipment:

- A bottle of carbonated water
- A 250 cm^3 beaker
- Universal indicator solution

(Continued)

(Continued)

- A tripod
- A gauze
- A heat-proof mat
- A Bunsen burner

Note: Universal indicator solution contains flammable material. Once it has been added to water, move the stock bottle well away from the Bunsen flame.

Method

Pour 100 cm³ carbonated water into the beaker. Add universal indicator to the water and note the colour. Heat the beaker of water on the tripod and gauze, protecting the bench with the heat-proof mat.

  As the acid solution is heated, the carbonic acid decomposes, the solution becomes less acidic and the universal indicator goes through the range of colours from reddish pink to green.

Verdigris

Copper does not react with water but with oxygen in the air. It slowly reacts with oxygen to form copper oxide. This oxide is capable of reacting with atmospheric carbon dioxide and other pollutants. When copper is exposed to air over a period of time, a green patina or coating is formed called verdigris. The name 'verdigris' comes from the French *vert-de-Grèce*, a green pigment originally imported from Greece. It is a complex mixture of copper compounds, including copper acetate and copper carbonate.

  Brass and bronze, which contain copper, can be cleaned with household materials to remove the verdigris. Lemons, ketchup and Worcestershire sauce have pH values less than 7. They are acidic but not too strongly acidic. Rubbing a little sauce or juice on to a weathered patch of metal creates a chemical reaction which dissolves the verdigris.

Engaging activity

Cement and neutralization

Apparatus

For this activity you will need the following equipment:

- A grapefruit-sized lump of concrete
- A hammer
- Safety spectacles
- Phenolphthalein solution

Method

Take the lump of concrete. Pour phenolphthalein solution (highly flammable) over the lump. Nothing will happen. Place the lump of concrete on the floor and, wearing eye protection, hit it hard with a hammer so that it breaks open. Quickly pour phenolphthalein over the newly exposed surface. The concrete goes bright pink, indicating that the inside of the concrete is a base.

Cement is made by roasting clay with calcium carbonate. Some of the calcium carbonate undergoes thermal decomposition to produce calcium oxide and carbon dioxide (which escapes as a gas). The calcium oxide remains in the cement, making it quite strongly basic.

Adding water to make concrete turns the calcium oxide into calcium hydroxide, a strong alkali. As concrete sets, any calcium hydroxide on the surface reacts with atmospheric carbon dioxide to reform calcium carbonate:

$$Ca(OH)_2 \text{ (s)} + CO_2 \text{ (g)} \rightarrow CaCO_3 \text{ (s)} + H_2O \text{ (l)}$$

The surface of concrete gives a colourless (neutral) result when tested with phenolphthalein. However, carbon dioxide penetrates, and neutralizes, the concrete only very slowly. This process is known as concrete carbonation. The inner alkaline concrete turns phenolphthalein purple/pink. The depth of carbon dioxide penetration can be seen by looking for a thin layer of colourless material between the exposed surface and the pink-stained inner concrete.

The rate of carbonation depends on many factors, but age is important:

$$\text{Depth of carbonation (mm)} \propto \text{(Age in years) } 0.5$$

Alkalis in buildings

Acid rain

Although, as outlined above, rainwater is naturally slightly acidic, the production of other gases by human activity can significantly increase the acid content of rainwater. One major source of additional acidity in rainwater is the sulphur impurities present in fossil fuels. When these impurities are burnt they release sulphur dioxide into the atmosphere:

$$S \text{ (s)} + O_2 \text{ (g)} \rightarrow SO_2 \text{ (g)}$$

This sulphur dioxide can then dissolve in rainwater to produce sulphurous acid:

$$SO_2 \text{ (g)} + H_2O \text{ (l)} \rightarrow H_2SO_3 \text{ (aq)}$$

The sulphur dioxide can also react with oxygen in the atmosphere to form sulphur trioxide, which dissolves to form sulphuric acid:

$$2SO_2 \text{ (g)} + O_2 \text{ (g)} \rightarrow 2SO_3 \text{ (g)}$$

This sulphur dioxide can then dissolve in rainwater to produce sulphurous acid:

$$SO_3 \text{ (g)} + H_2O \text{ (l)} \rightarrow H_2SO_4 \text{ (aq)}$$

Oxides of nitrogen (NO_x)

Although relatively unreactive, at the high temperatures (approximately 1000 °C) and pressures within an internal combustion engine, nitrogen will react with oxygen in the air to produce a range of different oxides. A general term to describe these oxides is NO_x. These oxides of nitrogen also dissolve in rainwater to give nitric acid, which increases its acidic nature. Nitrogen dioxide (NO_2) also acts as a catalyst in the formation of sulphur trioxide, so its effect on acid rain production is increased.

Acid rain can affect the following:

- **Forests**: Trees hundreds of miles away in Sweden and Germany can be damaged by acid rain stemming from the UK.
- **Fish**: Many lakes in Norway and Sweden now have no fish in them at all, not as a direct result of acid rain but indirectly by the acids dissolving otherwise insoluble aluminium compounds from the soil which are then washed into lakes where they poison the fish.
- **Buildings and metal structures**: Acid rain slowly dissolves metal structures and calcium carbonate-based building materials (limestone, marble and chalk are all different forms of calcium carbonate).

Strategies to combat the production of acid rain

The gases causing acid rain can be neutralized before they escape from the power station chimneys by reacting them with powdered calcium hydroxide or calcium carbonate, forming calcium sulphate. The calcium sulphate can be used to make plaster for the building industry.

Sulphur compounds can be removed from petrol and diesel fuel before being sold, which prevents the formation of sulphur dioxide and sulphur trioxide, but this makes the fuel more expensive. Currently in the UK a lower tax is imposed on these 'clean' fuels in order to offset the cost to the motorist and to encourage petrol manufacturers to produce more environmentally friendly fuels.

By using rhodium metal in the catalytic converter of a car's exhaust system the oxides of nitrogen are converted back into harmless nitrogen and oxygen. However rhodium (as well as platinum, which converts carbon monoxide into carbon dioxide and unused hydrocarbons into carbon dioxide and water) is expensive and this increases the cost of car manufacture. Lead compounds used to be added to petrol to increase engine performance. However, any traces of lead compounds in a car's exhaust gases are adsorbed on to the catalyst's surface, which renders the catalytic converter useless. This is called catalytic poisoning.

Acid soils

Depending on the nature of the underlying bedrock, a soil may be acidic or alkaline. Some plants are better suited to growing in acidic soils and will thrive in these conditions, whereas others are better suited to alkaline conditions. For example, azaleas, cranberries, heathers, maple trees and rhododendrons prefer acid conditions, while apples, birches, cabbages, cherries, hollies and plums grow better in alkaline soils. Most garden centres sell simple test kits to check the pH of soils.

It is possible to adjust the pH of soil by adding a carefully controlled amount of a weak acid or alkali. The most common way of combating acidity in soils is to add lime and gardeners, for example, sometimes sprinkle a little lime around cabbage plants when they are planted out. Farmers often need to resort to the same approach but on a larger scale, and this accounts for the large piles of white solid sometimes seen in farmers' fields in springtime. These piles are lime waiting to be spread on the soil prior to planting a commercial crop.

Insect stings: facts or old wives' tales?

It is often stated that the venom in a wasp sting is alkaline and therefore can be neutralized with vinegar (ethanoic acid) and that the neutralization reduces the pain. Similarly, a bee sting is said to be acidic and therefore an appropriate treatment would be to neutralize the sting with bicarbonate of soda (sodium hydrogencarbonate). Are these statements true?

It is true that bee venom contains formic (methanoic) acid, as do ant stings, and that wasp stings are alkaline. However, these are not the only active ingredients that cause the pain. Neutralizing a sting with either vinegar or bicarbonate of soda is unlikely to be effective or even possible because bee and wasp venom is injected beneath the skin's surface and it spreads much deeper into the tissues below. Pouring large volumes of unknown concentration acid or alkali solutions on to the skin's surface is unlikely even to reach the sting, so no neutralization is likely to occur.

The amount of venom injected by a bee or wasp is tiny (5–50 micrograms of fluid) in comparison with the large volumes of acid or alkali poured on to the skin so, again, no neutralization is likely to occur. However, this is not to say that the treatment does not work because rubbing the affected area distracts the mind from the pain and also, if you believe that a treatment will work, then it often will do – a case of psychology sometimes being more effective than chemistry.

Further reading

www.carlsberggroup.com/Company/Research/Pages/pHValue.aspx
This web page outlines how Sørensen devised the pH scale.

www.cfsan.fda.gov/~comm/lacf-phs.html
The US Food and Drug Administration's web page about acidified and low-acid canned foods.

www.germann.org/Products/Deep Purple/
This website outlines how deep purple and rainbow indicator are used to determine the depth of carbonation in concrete.

www.concrete-testing.com/chemical_analysis.htm
This website explains how the chemical analysis of concrete can provide information on the causes of concrete failure.

Section 3   Light and motion

In this section, of three chapters, you will be introduced to the science of:

- visible light;
- electric motors;
- rockets; and
- projectile motion.

This links to, and will help you deliver, the various national curricula for England, Ireland, Scotland and Wales as set out below.

By working through this section it is expected that you will be able to describe and explain:

- light as a wave, and reflection and refraction;
- magnetic fields around electrical wires and the construction of simple motors; and
- distance, time and speed, and the analysis of a projectile's trajectory.

Please turn over to see how this section relates to your curriculum.

National Curriculum for England	Junior Certificate Science Syllabus	Environmental Studies – Society, Science and Technology	Science in the National Curriculum for Wales
KS3 Energy, electricity and forces **b** forces are interactions between objects and can affect their shape and motion **KS4:** **7b** energy, electricity and radiations ... electrical power is readily transferred and controlled, and can be used in a range of different situations **7c** radiations, including ionising radiations, can transfer energy **7d** radiations in the form of waves can be used for communication	**3B3** Light **3B4** Reflection of light, refraction of light **3A1** Perform simple calculations [including] speed, velocity and acceleration **3C3** Current, electricity, voltage [including] magnetic effects of an electric current	Properties and uses of energy: Developing an understanding of energy through the study of the properties and uses of heat, light, sound and electricity Energy and forces: Developing an understanding of forces and how they can explain familiar phenomena and practices Energy and forces: Describe the structure and function of an electromagnet	**KS3:** **1.12** How electromagnets are constructed and used in devices **2.1** How distance, time and speed can be determined and represented graphically **2.3** The forces acting on familiar moving objects **3** Waves; the behaviour of light **KS4** Waves; the characteristics of waves

7 Looking at light

Gren Ireson

This chapter covers:

- light as a wave
- the electromagnetic spectrum
- reflection and refraction
- total internal reflection
- dispersion, interference and diffraction.

 Test your own knowledge

Before reading the material in this chapter test your current knowledge with the following questions:

1. In what ways can we say light and sound are a) similar; b) different?
2. Sometimes you may hear people talk of light 'bouncing off' a surface, such as water. What is the correct term?
3. When light travels from the air into, for example, a block of glass it changes direction. What do we call this effect?
4. What happens to the speed of the light as it goes a) from air to glass; b) from glass to air?
5. What is the correct term for the effect we see when colours appear on the back of a CD or when we see a rainbow?

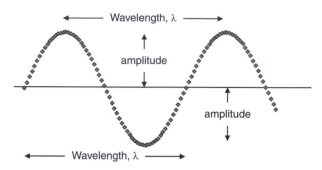

Figure 7.1   Wave basics

Wave basics

Light is a wave which belongs to a large family of waves called electro-magnetic radiation. All electromagnetic waves share the same properties:

- They all travel at the same speed in air (technically in a vacuum but the difference is very small) – 300,000,000 ms⁻¹ or 3×10^8 ms⁻¹. Sometimes this is simply called the speed of light.
- They can all be reflected, although you have to use different materials.
- They can all be refracted, although you have to use different materials.
- They can all be diffracted, although you have to use different materials.
- The speed of electromagnetic waves is given by: Speed = Frequency × Wavelength, or $v = f\lambda$.
- They travel in straight lines although the directions of these lines change as they pass from one material to another.

In this chapter we explore the above terms giving you both the theory, to help you feel confident in your own subject knowledge, and teaching ideas, to help make your lessons more engaging.

When we talk about a wave we need to understand the basic terms that describe it (see Figure 7.1):

- **Wavelength** (measured in metre, m) is the distance between two, consecutive, identical points on the wave (e.g. crest to crest). The symbol used for wavelength is the Greek letter λ, pronounced lambda.
- **Frequency** (measured in Hertz, Hz) is the number of complete wavelengths passing a fixed point in one second.
- **Amplitude** is the maximum displacement from the centre. This tells us about the energy carried by the wave.

Table 7.1 *The electromagnetic spectrum*

Type	Wavelength	Frequency	Typical Application
Gamma rays	10^{-12} m	3×10^{20} Hz	Sterilization of medical instruments; destroying cancerous cells
X-rays	10^{-10} m	3×10^{18} Hz	Medical imaging; dental; broken bones
Ultraviolet	10^{-8} m	3×10^{16} Hz	Detecting security markers; hardening some dental coatings
Visible light	10^{-7} m	3×10^{15} Hz	Seeing! Some wavelengths are vital for photosynthesis
Infrared	10^{-5} m	3×10^{13} Hz	Communications; data and television via 'cable'
Microwaves	10^{-2} m	3×10^{10} Hz	Cooking; mobile telephones
Radio waves	Up to 10^{4} m	3×10^{4} Hz	Radio and television signals

When we talk about wavelength we are describing the length after which the wave starts to repeat itself. This is much the same as with sound but, whereas with sound, which humans can hear, the wavelength is between 15 mm and 15 m, wavelengths for electromagnetic waves range from 10^{-12} m to 10^{4} m. For visible light (i.e. the light humans can detect) the wavelength ranges over a very narrow band from 4×10^{-7} m to 7.5×10^{-7} m. This is more often written as 400 nm to 750 nm (1 nm = 1 'nano' metre; 'nano' is 10^{-9} m, more Greek just like lambda).

The extent of the electromagnetic spectrum, as this family of waves is known, can be better seen in Table 7.1. The figures in Table 7.1 can be derived using the relationship between speed, frequency and length:

$$v = f\lambda$$

For example all electromagnetic waves travel at 3×10^{8} ms^{-1} and, for ultraviolet, we have a wavelength of 3×10^{-8} m. The equation becomes:

$$f = \frac{v}{\lambda}$$

which gives us:

$$f = \frac{300\,000\,000}{0.00000003} = 10^{16} \text{Hz}$$

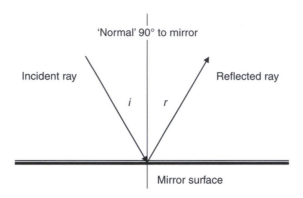

Figure 7.2   Reflection at a mirror surface

Reflection of light

When we read a text, like this one, this is made possible by the fact that light is 'hitting' the page and being reflected into our eyes. The same is true when we look in a mirror. For visible light any glossy surface will act as a good reflector, but a small piece of mirrored glass is the best option.

What is often called the 'law of reflection' states that the angle between the normal and the incident ray, the angle of incidence, is always equal to the angle between the normal and the reflected ray, the angle of reflection

If a narrow ray of light is directed towards a mirror it is reflected as shown in Figure 7.2, but don't take our word for it – try it yourself. While Figure 7.2 correctly explains what is happening and the results you or your students would get, many students, especially younger ones, find constructing the normal difficult and fail to see its significance. We would suggest that, when dealing with a plane, flat, surface, the normal can be omitted and the simplified approach given in Figure 7.3 be used.

Angle *i* always equals angle *r*. Snooker players and squash players make good use of this.

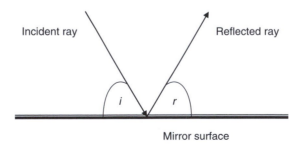

Figure 7.3   Simplified reflection

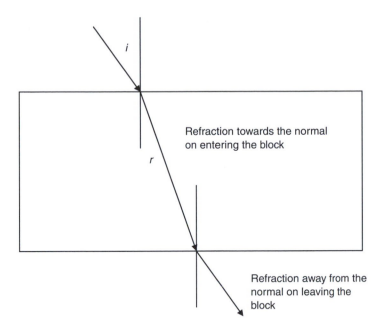

Refraction towards the normal on entering the block

Refraction away from the normal on leaving the block

Figure 7.4   Refraction in a rectangular block

Refraction of light

When light passes from one material, or medium, to another, it changes direction at the boundary. This is why swimming pools look less deep than they are and why a straw in a drink looks 'bent' when viewed from the side. This phenomenon is known as refraction and can be easily demonstrated at school level.

If you were to direct a narrow ray of light towards a transparent block (for example, perspex or glass), then you would observe something similar to that shown in Figure 7.4. Again, we hope you don't take our word for it; there is no substitute for trying it. *Points to note*: The rays only change direction at the boundary. The ray entering the block is parallel to the one leaving.

We would also advocate that you don't tell your students this but, rather, let them investigate. This approach allows you to pose two questions: what happens if the ray of light is directed along the normal? And if you have higher-level students, can you find a relationship between the incident angle and refracted angle?

We leave you to answer the first question but the second is a little more tricky, and the students may need some guidance. If the students measure angle *i* and angle *r* over a range of values of *i*, then they can be guided towards:

Angle *i*	Angle *r*	Sin *i*	Sin *r*	Sin *i*/Sin *r*
				This column gives a constant value

The numerical value given in the final column is called the refractive index of the material. The larger the value the greater the amount of refraction. If two materials, with identical refractive indices, are in contact with each other, then no refraction takes place.

All lenses rely on refraction and, since our eyes do a great deal of refraction at the cornea, this explains why we find it difficult to see under water. The refractive index of water and the cornea are almost the same and, hence, little refraction takes places, making it difficult for us to focus.

Earlier in this section we mentioned that refraction is responsible for the apparent depth of water looking less than the real depth. Look at Figure 7.5. Our eyes operate on the fact that light travels in straight lines and, therefore, as shown in Figure 7.5, they think the light is coming from nearer the surface than is true.

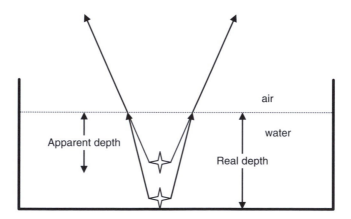

Figure 7.5   Real and apparent depth

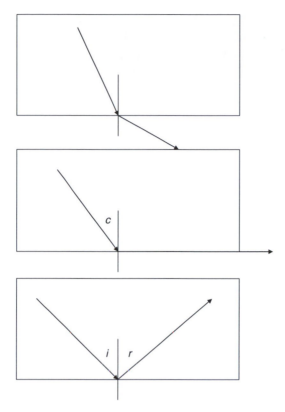

Figure 7.6   Critical angle

Total internal reflection (TIR)

We have seen that when light enters a transparent material it is refracted and that the same is true when it leaves the block. However, if the angle between the normal and the internal edge is greater than a given value, then something strange happens.

   If we consider a glass block with a ray of light incident on the internal edge, then we would observe the light behaving as in Figure 7.6, but please, as always, don't take our word for it. In the first diagram every-thing is behaving as expected and as previously observed. In the second diagram, when the angle is at the critical angle, c, then the ray of light would try to run along the edge of the block. For glass the critical angle is of the order of 42° but it does vary with the type of glass, and this can make for an investigation in schools. In the third diagram the situation becomes identical to what you already know about reflection. This is known as total internal reflection, or TIR.

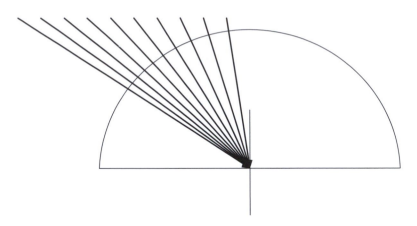

Figure 7.7   Finding the critical angle

Measuring the angle inside the block can be tricky and so we would suggest the following approach be used in schools, but, to keep it interesting, don't tell your students what to expect before they carry out the investigation. Figure 7.7 gives the investigation set-up, and the students should be asked to predict what they expect to happen when a ray of light is directed down each line in turn. Only then should they carry out the investigation and record their observations.

Before starting the investigation with your class, you need to prepare the template as shown in Figure 7.7 by drawing around a semi-circular transparent block and marking lines in five-degree steps. This means the students don't have to try measuring angles inside the block.

Why is it that, when the ray of light enters the block through the curved surface, no refraction takes places (think about the earlier work in this chapter)? The students should be able to observe that the light is refracted up to a certain line and then TIR occurs. The critical angle lies between these two lines, and some students could be tasked with plotting 1° lines between the two markers to refine their value.

While this is fun to do it does have important and far-reaching applications, from simple reflectors on primary students' coats to medical investigations and communications technology. Simple reflectors may look flat but are made of tiny 'corner cubes' which ensure that light entering them is sent back the way it came from. This can be seen in Figure 7.8.

Since we know that light travels in straight lines we obviously can't make it go around corners, or can we? The so-called optical fibres, as used in medical investigations, do just that by repeated TIR. This can be shown, simply, as in Figure 7.9.

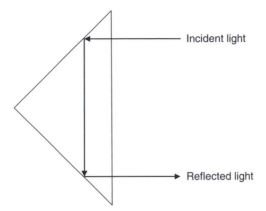

Figure 7.8   Corner cube

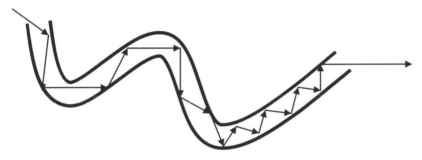

Figure 7.9   Fibre optic

How science works

Before continuing with our work on light let's take a little break to see how the topic of light can be applied to How Science Works. Within the How Science Works requirements the students should investigate how scientific thinking has changed over time.

We accept now that light is a wave and part of a broader family of waves, electromagnetic waves, as discussed earlier in this chapter. However it was not always so, and Newton thought light was made of little 'balls' which he called *corpuscles*. A Dutch scientist, Christiaan Huygens, suggested that light was a wave but, at the time, given Newton's fame, most scientists believed him. Newton's theory, however, couldn't explain refraction. His theory would have

(Continued)

(Continued)

had light refracting away from the normal when it enters the glass, and so correctly and eventually Huygens' views became accepted.

The students could be asked to research the two men and their ideas on light, looking at the evidence used to arrive at our current understanding. Or, if the students are able, they could role play the two men debating their theories, with the remainder of the class being a *scientific audience*.

Dispersion, interference and diffraction

In terms of observation, these phenomena are simple, but the explanatory theory can be difficult and goes beyond what is generally required in a programme of study up to the age of 16 in UK schools.

Dispersion refers to the separating out of the colours that make up *white light*. Newton is credited with the first demonstration of the fact that light from the Sun, white light, is in fact made up of a mixture of colours. Just as visible light is part of the electromagnetic spectrum, then light has its own spectrum. Newton reported seven colours, but the human eye is very insensitive to indigo and at least one of the authors of this book can never see more than five. The simplest set-up for this, using a prism, is shown in Figure 7.10.

For the students, an aide-memoire to remember the order of the colours is Richard Of York Gave Battle In Vain. Violet Bends Most Violently might help them to remember that violet is at the bottom, as shown in Figure 7.10.

Recalling what you know about the refraction of light and the wavelength of waves, this can be explained by the fact that each colour has a different wavelength and that the prism has a different refractive index for each wavelength. You will have seen this spectrum when you see

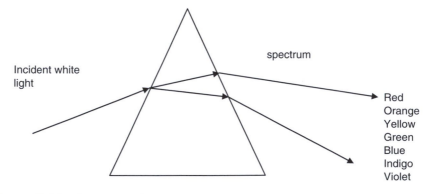

Figure 7.10 Spectrum of white light

a rainbow or when a raindrop acts like a prism. Again, we see a spectrum of colours, but can you see seven?

Interference and diffraction are more advanced topics when studying waves, but their effects can be seen in the colours on the back of a CD, in oil on water and on peacock feathers. While not covering the theory here we are offering an activity that allows the students to *capture a rainbow*.

Engaging activities

While some standard practical activities for the students to carry out in school are described earlier in this chapter, what follows are two activities the students could easily reproduce at home.

Capturing 'rainbows'

Submerge a small piece of black sugar paper in a shallow tray filled with a few centimetres of water. Pipette one or two drops of clear nail varnish on to the surface of the water (see Figure 7.11). You should see an interference pattern (i.e. a series of coloured fringes) as the nail varnish forms a thin film on the water's surface.

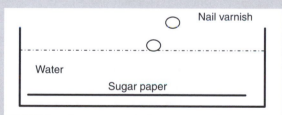

Figure 7.11   Capturing 'rainbows'

Carefully lift the sugar paper, keeping it flat if possible. The film will adhere to the sugar paper and, when dry, can be stuck into the students' books. The interference pattern will remain.

Trapping light in a stream of water

We have looked at TIR and its application to fibre optics. The same effect can be achieved using a laser pointer and a stream of water. The water acts as an optical fibre and the light follows the stream as it changes direction.

Using a 1 litre soft drink bottle, made of clear plastic (see Figure 7.12), make a small hole a few centimetres from the bottom (a 5 mm cork borer works well). Place your finger over the hole and completely fill the bottle. Replace the cap and the water will stay in the bottle when you uncover the hole. Can you explain this?

(Continued)

(Continued)

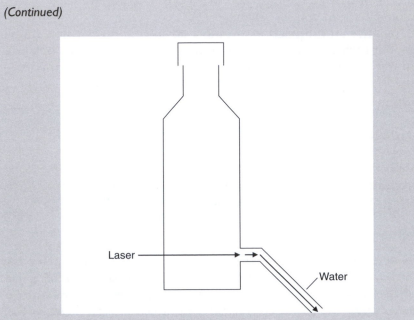

Figure 7.12 Trapping light in a stream of water

Position the laser pointer, or laser if you have access to one, on the opposite side to the hole such that the light emerges through the hole. Release the cap. The water will now run out and the light will follow the path of the water, so make sure it is positioned to flow into a sink!

Further reading

Breithaupt, J. (2006) *AQA Physics*. Cheltenham: Nelson Thornes.

Ross, K., Lakin, L. and Callaghan, P. (2006) *Teaching Secondary Science*. London: David Foulton.

Wood-Robinson, V. (2006) *ASE Guide to Secondary Science Education*. Hatfield ASE.
  These texts are general physics texts and include good chapters on light, waves and the electromagnetic spectrum.

www.qca.org.uk/qca_9437.aspx
  This is the QCA website which links to all aspects of How Science Works.

www.practicalphysics.org/go/HowScienceWorks.html
  This practical physics site offers a series of links to case studies and example practical work to help with How Science Works in the classroom.

8 Electric motors

Mark Crowley

This chapter covers:

- the magnetic fields around electrical wires
- Maxwell's Screw Rule
- Fleming's Left Hand Rule
- using currents and magnetic fields to create motion
- the construction of simple electrical motors.

Test your own knowledge

Before reading the material in this chapter test your current knowledge with the following questions:

1. Although we cannot see the field lines around a magnet, we can detect them using a plotting compass (see Figure 8.1). Where around a magnet are field lines most concentrated?
2. Do field lines point from North to South or South to North?
3. A magnetic field is produced when an electric current flows through a coil of wire. What will happen to an electromagnet when a) the current is switched off; b) the current is reversed?
4. True or false? The following steps will make an electromagnet stronger: a) wrapping the coil around an iron core; b) using less turns to the coil; c) increasing the current flowing through the coil.
5. Electric motors contain electromagnets. What energy changes occur inside an electric motor?

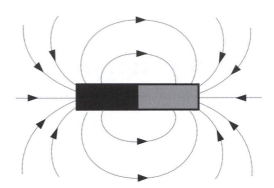

Figure 8.1   Field lines around a permanent magnet

Motors and magnets

Consider the following electrical items: DVD players, escalators, food processors, electric windows and microwave cookers. They all contain motors designed to convert electrical energy into kinetic (mechanical) energy. This conversion of energy relies on the interaction of magnetic fields.

A magnet is an object that produces a magnetic field. Some materials that are strongly affected by magnetic fields include iron, cobalt and nickel. These materials can themselves be magnetized and may form a permanent magnet once exposed to a magnetic field. It is possible to create temporary magnets. An electromagnet only exhibits magnetic properties while an electric current passes through it; it loses its magnetic behaviour when the current stops.

How science works

Scientists often seek to explain different natural phenomena within a single theory. In investigating a possible connection between electricity, heat and light, a new branch of science was discovered – at the time it was called 'electrodynamics' but we now know it as 'electromagnetism'.

In 1729, the English scientist, Stephen Gray, discovered and investigated electric currents, conductors and insulators. Hans Christian Ørsted, a Danish scientist, was demonstrating the heating effect of an electric current during a public lecture in 1819. He observed that a nearby compass needle was deflected as the neighbouring electric circuit was switched on and off (see Figure 8.2).

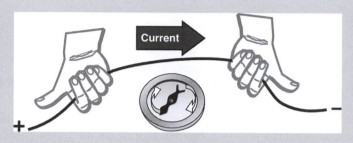

Figure 8.2   Deflection of a magnet by an electric current

The effect observed was small but encouraged Ørsted to follow a new series of experiments. After several months of experimenting, Ørsted had sufficient, convincing results to publish his work in Latin – the common language of scientists at the time. André-Marie Ampère read Ørsted's report and began to check the work by repeating the same experiments. Ampère quickly improved the description of the effect with his own mathematical equation, which connected the strength of the magnetic field to the size of the current and distance from the wire.

Further advances in the field of electromagnetism were made by the English scientist, Michael Faraday. He was able to use the circular nature of the magnetic fields around electrical conductors to create circular motion and, later, to develop apparatus for electromagnetic induction.

Practical activity

Magnetic field around a single wire

Apparatus

For this activity you will need the following equipment:

- A stand and clamp
- Copper wire, enamelled, 26 swg, 50–100 cm with bare ends
- White cardboard
- Plotting compasses
- A power supply, low voltage
- Optional: iron filings

(Continued)

(Continued)

Method

Clamp the white cardboard horizontally and arrange the equipment as shown in Figure 8.3. Switch on the power supply and sprinkle iron filings on to the white board. Tap the board gently – a pattern of concentric circles should develop. Switch off the supply. Remove the iron filings. Place small plotting compasses around the wire (see Figure 8.3). Reverse the supply connections to see what effect this has on the compass needles.

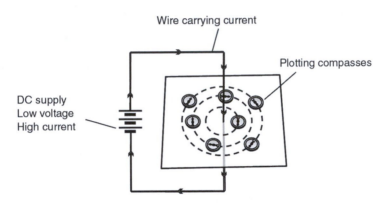

Figure 8.3   Mapping out magnetic field lines around a conductor

Maxwell's screw rule

The previous experiment demonstrates the concentric nature of the field lines around a conductor carrying a current. The direction of the magnetic field lines can be determined by Maxwell's Screw Rule, or the Right Hand Grip Rule.

Imagine a right-handed screw pointing in the same the direction as an electric current (see Figure 8.4). When the screw is turned to follow the current, it will rotate in the same direction as the magnetic field around the current. If you pointed the thumb of your right hand in the direction of the current (I) and gripped the wire with the rest of your hand, your fingers will curve around the wire in the same direction as the field (B).

The strength of the magnetic field formed by such a conductor depends on the magnitude of the current. A stronger current flowing through the conductor produces a stronger magnetic field – this is shown by a greater concentration of field lines close to the wire.

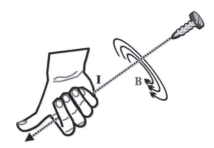

Figure 8.4   Right-hand rule for electromagnetic fields

Practical activity

Jumping wire demonstration

Apparatus

For this activity you will need the following equipment:

* A length of insulated copper wire, 26 swg, 50 cm with bare ends
* Two stands, a boss and a clamp
* A 3–5 V power supply
* A switch, crocodile clips and connectors
* A powerful horseshoe or ceramic block (alternatively you could use a pile of several neodymium magnets)

Method

Place the wire between the poles of a ceramic/horseshoe magnet as shown in Figure 8.5. The wire needs to be slack and loosely gripped by the clamps (use rubber-coated clamps where possible).

Start by experimenting with a low voltage (2 V). When the switch is closed, the wire should jump into the air and stay suspended until the switch is released.

Do not keep the switch held down for a long time. The wire is acting as a short circuit and will quickly build up a high temperature. A short pulse of electricity should be enough to demonstrate the effect. Reverse the electrical contacts and demonstrate how the wire moves when the current is reversed.

Alternatively, suspend a 20 cm length of aluminium foil (2 cm wide) between the poles of a strong horseshoe magnet. Make sure that the foil is slack and able to move up and down. Once a low-voltage power source is applied to either ends of the foil, it will move in a similar way to the 'jumping wire'.

(Continued)

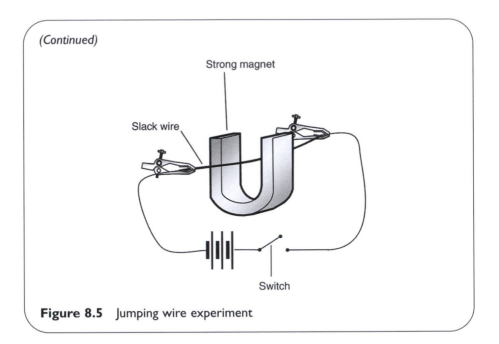

Figure 8.5 Jumping wire experiment

Fleming's left hand rule

Magnetic fields run from the north to the south poles of a magnet. In the previous activity the wire runs at 90° (perpendicular) to this field. The magnetic field created by the electrical current interacts with the field flowing between the poles of the permanent magnet. The result is a force which moves the wire upward.

The size of the force can be increased by increasing:

- the magnetic field strength;
- the length of the wire in the field; and
- the current in the wire.

Fleming's Left Hand Rule provides a way of determining the direction of a force on a current-carrying conductor in a magnetic field. Using your left hand, align the first finger in the direction of the magnetic field and the second finger in the direction of the current in the wire. Moving your thumb at 90° to both these fingers will mean you are pointing in the direction of the force on the conductor (see Figure 8.6).

There is a simple way to remember these:

- First finger: Field.
- seCond finger: Current.
- thuMb: Motion (or Thumb: Thrust).

Figure 8.6 Fleming's left hand rule

Engaging activities

Simple homopolar motors

A motor is a device that converts one form of energy (electrical, chemical) into movement. In the following activity, electrical energy is used to cause rotation.

In most electrical motors, a coil sits in a magnetic field formed between two different poles. As a current passes through the coil, the magnetic field it forms interacts with the surrounding field causing the motor to rotate. Electrical contacts, called commutators and brushes, are arranged so that the current passing through the coil changes direction as the motor spins – every half turn of the motor the current inside the coil is reversed. These motors are referred to as brushed DC electric motors.

Activities to build brushed electric motors can be enjoyable but they are time consuming. Motors that are much simpler and just as enjoyable to build include homopolar motors. The homopolar motor has a fixed magnetic field: it does not change direction or strength. In these motors the magnetic field usually points along the axis of rotation.

Table-top homopolar motor

Apparatus

For this activity you will need the following equipment:

- An AA battery
- One or two neodymium magnets (we suggest magnets which are 12 × 6 mm (diameter × height) with a nickel surface. This will allow the magnet to conduct electricity and the wire to move easily around the magnet.

(Continued)

(Continued)

- Copper wire (18 gauge)
- Pliers

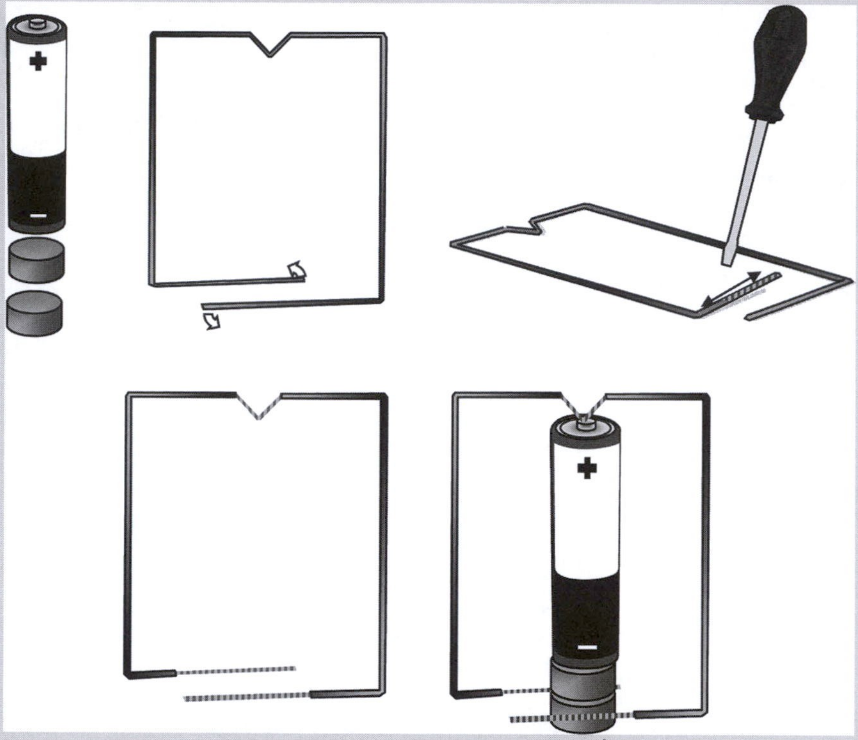

Figure 8.7 Making a simple homopolar motor

Method

Place the neodymium magnet(s) on the negative terminal of the battery. Bend the wire to form the rectangular shape shown in Figure 8.7. Form a V shape in the top edge of the wire. This dent will eventually rest on top of the positive terminal of the battery.

The copper might be insulated with enamel. You will need to remove the enamel/varnish from both ends of the wire and in the V-shaped contact. Balance the copper wire on top of the battery. The free ends of the wire may need to be adjusted so that they form a good contact with the magnets and without gripping the base too tightly.

Once the motor starts to rotate, the top contact might wobble and fall off the terminal. Try different V shapes so that the contact remains in place but able to spin freely. (Adding a dent to the battery's terminal often helps.)

This motor is designed to sit on top of a table, but there are alternative designs in which the battery is held in the hand. Since the copper wire creates a short circuit, draining the battery quickly, the wires in either design can become quite hot.

Handheld homopolar motor

Apparatus

For this activity you will need the following equipment:

- A D-sized battery
- One neodymium magnet
- A short length of wire
- A nail or screw
- A short length of straw (optional)

(See Figure 8.8 for the way to assemble this equipment.)

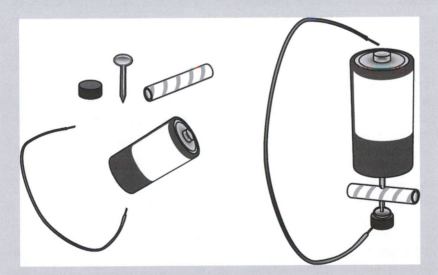

Figure 8.8 An alternative homopolar motor

These simple motors contain a single strand of wire, whereas most electric motors contain a coil. The following details show how another simple motor can be built with a coil (still without commutators or brushes).

(Continued)

(Continued)

Coil homopolar motor

Apparatus

For this activity you will need the following equipment:

- Two AA batteries and a holder
- Four crocodile clips and wires
- One neodymium magnet
- Enamelled copper wire (18 gauge)
- A connection block
- Two paper clips
- A screwdriver
- A test tube (or other small cylinder)

Method

(See Figure 8.9.) Straighten out a paper clip and bend one end to form a capital **N**. This may require a pair of pliers. Repeat with the second paper clip. Loosen the screws on either side of the connection block. Feed the straight end of the paper clip through the connection block so that 2 cm sticks out at the opposite side. Tighten both screws to hold it in place.

Use a piece of Blu-Tack or Plasticine under the block to fix it to the table. The block and paper clips form the cradle of the motor. Wind the copper wire around a test tube to make a coil. Do not wind all the wire into a coil – leave 4–5 cm of free (unwound) wire on either end of the coil. Stop the coil from unwinding by wrapping one free end around the coil three times. Repeat with the other free end directly opposite the other free end.

Place the coil on a flat surface. Leaving the underside of the wire untouched, scratch off the enamel from only the topside of the two free ends. Place the coil into the arms of the cradle. Check that the coil spins freely. If necessary adjust the cradle's arms so that the coil remains in the middle as it spins.

Attach the crocodile clip/wires to the ends of paper clips protruding from the connection block. Connect these wires to the power supply/batteries' terminals.

Bring the neodymium magnet close to the coil. The coil usually stays horizontal and may need a quick flick to help it to start to rotate. Once the coil starts to spin it should continue, quickly, 'under its own steam'.

If the magnet is held on the end of screwdriver it becomes easier to feel the interaction between the electromagnet and neodymium magnet. Someone holding on to the screwdriver will feel a 'pulse' as the electromagnet spins.

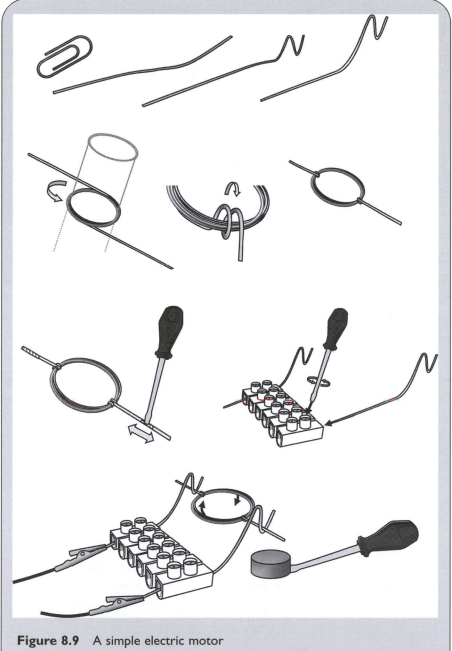

Figure 8.9   A simple electric motor

(Continued)

(Continued)

The electromagnet is only active for half its spin. As the coil spins in the arms of the cradle, either enamel-coated wire or exposed metal comes into contact with the paper clip arms. When the exposed metal touches the cradle's arms a current flows through the coil: the coil becomes temporarily electromagnetic. This interacts with the neodymium magnet causing either repulsion or attraction according to the direction of the current flowing through the coil.

The coil turns around in response to this repulsive/attractive force. The exposed metal spins around so that the enamel coating comes into contact with the metallic arm. No current flows and the electromagnet is switched off. The coil continues to turn, due to its inertia, and once again becomes an electromagnet.

Further reading

Baigrie, B.S. (2007) *Electricity and Magnetism: A Historical Perspective.* Westport, CT: Greenwood Press.

This readable book covers the central concepts of electricity and magnetism and how scientific understanding has developed from ancient times to the early twentieth century. It is intended for students as well as the general reader.

Fairley, P. (2007) *Electricity and Magnetism (Great Ideas of Science).* Breckenridge, CO: Twenty-first Century Books. An alternative book to Baigrie on the same subject. This book tells the story of scientists and their discoveries to explain how the theory of electromagnetism came to be.

http://chem.ch.huji.ac.il/history/electrochemists.htm

An interesting and useful website describing a number of scientists who contributed to the fields of electricity, electromagnetism, electrical technology, electronics, electrical telegraphy, radio and electrochemistry.

www.practicalphysics.org/go/Resources_13.html

An excellent online case study by David Sang of Ørsted's discovery and how each stage in Ørsted's work links into the concept of How Science Works.

9 Rockets

Mark Crowley

This chapter covers:

- distance, time and speed and the calculation of these quantities
- equations of motion
- experiments to determine the acceleration due to gravity
- the construction and use of an air missile launcher
- the analysis of a projectile's trajectory.

Test your own knowledge

Before reading the material in this chapter test your current knowledge with the following questions:

1. The path of a toy hovercraft was recorded over 10 seconds (a graph of distance against time is shown in Figure 9.1). When was the toy accelerating? At a steady speed? Decelerating?
2. How do you calculate the average speed of the toy?
3. The toy achieved a top speed of 2.5 m/s. Between which times did the toy achieve this higher speed?
4. Sketch a chart showing speed against time for the chart in Figure 9.1.
5. What is the difference between speed and velocity?

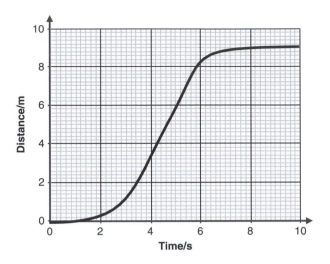

Figure 9.1   Distance–time graph for toy hovercraft

How science works

As scientists have collected experimental data, they have been able to support or refute ideas and theories. However, culture, politics and ethics have greatly influenced the ability of scientists to challenge current thinking. This was particularly true for Galileo Galilei.

The Greek philosopher, Aristotle (384–322 BC), developed a theory of 'gravity and levity' to explain the motion of different objects. Aristotle claimed that objects had a 'natural place' which they were drawn towards – the centre of the Earth for heavy objects and the heavenly spheres for gases. The speed of this motion was thought to be proportional to the mass of the object.

Between 1590 and 1608, Galileo Galilei (AD 1564–1642) developed mathematical formulae to describe the motion of falling objects and the parabolic arc of moving projectiles. Galileo used his results to suggest that unequal weights should fall in the same manner – with a uniform acceleration as long as the air resistance remained negligible.

Galileo also used the newly invented telescope to study the solar system and collected strong evidence for Nicholas Copernicus' heliocentric theory – positioning the sun at the centre of the moving planets. This was at odds with the Aristotle's geocentric (Earth at the centre) model which was strongly supported by the Catholic Church. In 1633 Galileo was ordered to Rome to stand trial on suspicion of heresy for publishing work which debated these ideas. He was required to recant his support for heliocentric ideas, placed under house arrest and forbidden from publishing of any of his works.

While under arrest, Galileo completed his mathematical description of falling objects (*Discourses and Mathematical Demonstrations Concerning the Two New Sciences*). This was smuggled out of Italy and taken to Holland, where it was published in 1638.

In 1971, on *Apollo 15*, the fourth Moon landing, Commander David Scott performed a live experiment on television. He dropped a geologic hammer and a falcon's feather at the same time from the same height. Both objects fell at the same rate, confirming Galileo's prediction of some 400 years earlier.

Mathematical treatment of motion

Speed is a scalar quantity. It represents the rate at which an object covers distance. Velocity is a vector quantity. It represents the rate at which an object changes its position. Velocity is important when direction (e.g. up, down) needs to be considered. The key equations are as follows:

$$\frac{\text{Average}}{\text{velocity}} = \frac{\text{Distance travelled}}{\text{Time taken}} \; \text{ms}^{-1}$$

$$\text{Acceleration} = \frac{\text{Change in velocity}}{\text{Time taken}} \; \text{ms}^{-2}$$

In terms of symbols, we commonly use the following:

$$s = \text{Distance travelled}$$
$$t = \text{Time taken}$$
$$v = \text{Final velocity}$$
$$u = \text{Initial velocity}$$
$$a = \text{(constant) Acceleration}$$

Note: Alphabetically, v comes after u. Hence final velocity (v) comes after initial velocity (u).

The *average* velocity of a moving object can be obtained from Distance ÷ Time *or* from the average (statistical mean) of final and initial velocities:

$$\frac{v + u}{2} = \frac{s}{t} \; \text{ms}^{-1}$$

Rearranging this equation gives:

$$t = \frac{2s}{v + u} \text{ s}$$

Similarly:

$$a = \frac{v - u}{t} \text{ ms}^{-2}$$

can be arranged to give:

$$t = \frac{v - u}{a} \text{ s}$$

Since 'time' has been made the subject of both equations, we can combine the two new equations to give:

$$\frac{v - u}{a} = \frac{2s}{v + u}$$

$$(v - u)(v + u) = 2as$$
$$v^2 - u^2 = 2as$$

An object dropped from rest has an initial velocity of zero ($u = 0$). If it experiences only the force gravity and no drag, it has predictable velocities at different points in its descent, regardless of its mass:

$$v^2 = 2 \times a \times s$$
$$v = \sqrt{(2 \times a \times s)} \text{ ms}^{-1}$$

and

$$a = \frac{v^2}{2s}$$

Where:

a = acceleration due to gravity (ms^{-2})
s = distance object has fallen (m)

Several experiments can be used to confirm a value for a by measuring velocities at different points in the decent of a falling object (g is commonly used to represent a when investigating acceleration due to gravity).

A common way to measure acceleration is to use light gates through which a moving object passes. In the example in Figure 9.2, a falling mass pulls a piece of black card (on top of a trolley) through two light gates. The card interrupts the first light gate for t_1 seconds and the

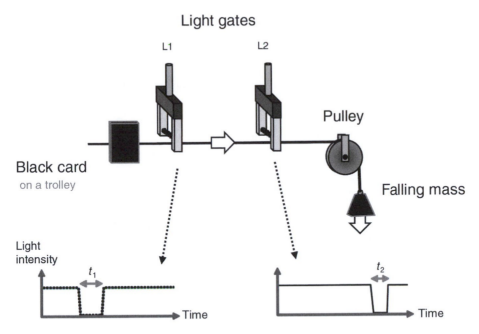

Figure 9.2 Determining g through data logging

second light gate for a shorter time of t_2 seconds. Once the width of the card and the distance between the gates are known, the timings can be turned into velocities and then, in turn, the change in velocity can be used to calculate the acceleration.

Inexpensive digital cameras, with a video function, offer another way of determining the acceleration due to gravity. The following activity outlines a method of collecting and analysing data on a falling object.

Practical activity

Digital table-tennis balls

Apparatus

For this activity you will need the following equipment:

- A digital camera/camcorder and a tripod
- A ruler or tape measure
- A table-tennis ball
- Video-editing software (see the 'Further reading and references' section at the end of this chapter)

(Continued)

(Continued)

Method

Capturing a video of the table-tennis ball falling in good light should be relatively easy. Consider where the person releasing the ball stands – they might cast a shadow over the ball. Have a reference object (of known dimensions) in the background – for example, a metre ruler. Use a dark background and position any source of illumination behind the camera. This will help to give a better contrast for the analysis of each frame.

Figure 9.3 shows the first five frames of the experiment from the point at which the ball was released. At a rate of 16 fps, each frame was recorded 0.0625 s apart (one sixteenth of a second). To capture each frame, the camera shutter opens for a fraction of a second (around one thirty-second of a second). The position of the ball is recorded. However, during the time that the shutter remains open, the ball falls further. This causes the blur. As the ball picks up speed, the blur increases.

Between the first and second frames (a gap of 0.0625 seconds), the ball falls by 1.9 cm. This distance is calculated by measuring the mid-point of the blurred ball. By analysing each frame (taking mid-points of the blurred ball), a distance time graph can be plotted (bottom of Figure 9.3).

We can convert each distance measurement into metres and calculate the *average* velocity (ms^{-1}) for each successive frame:

$$\frac{-0.019}{0.0625} = \textit{-0.30} \text{ ms}^{-1}$$

$$\frac{-0.057}{0.0625} = \textit{-0.91} \text{ ms}^{-1}$$

$$\frac{-0.096}{0.0625} = \textit{-1.54} \text{ ms}^{-1}$$

$$\frac{-0.135}{0.0625} = \textit{-2.16} \text{ ms}^{-1}$$

The velocities become more negative – there is acceleration downward due to gravity. From one frame to the next the velocity changes by approximately –0.6 ms^{-1}.

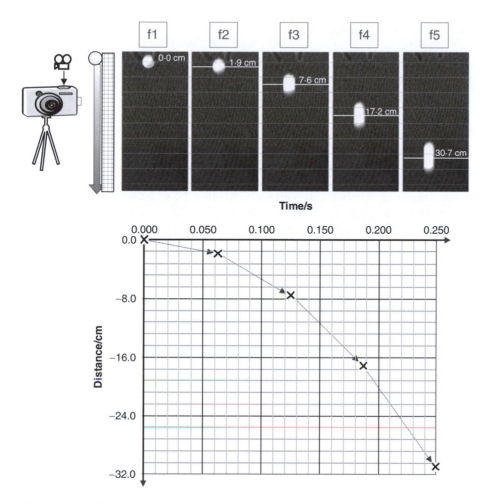

Figure 9.3 Determination of g by digital video

This regular change in velocity indicates a constant (uniform) force – in this case, gravity. We can use an average change in velocity (–0.62 ms⁻¹) to calculate the acceleration due to gravity:

$$\text{Acceleration} = -0.62 \text{ ms}^{-1} \div 0.0625 \text{ s}$$
$$= -9.8 \text{ ms}^{-2}$$

This particular example gives a value for acceleration due to gravity which closely matches the accepted value ($g = 9.81$ ms⁻²). However, this frame analysis method can yield a range of values (10 ± 3 ms⁻²). We often take a rough-and-ready value of 10 ms⁻² for g.

Rockets and projectiles

Rockets and projectiles are considered to be different objects. In both cases gases can be used to create forces that propel each type of object. A rocket is an object that obtains its own thrust by the ejection of exhaust material. A projectile is an object propelled by a force that ceases after launch. Once an object has been launched or fired, the path it follows is known as its trajectory. Trajectories are influenced by gravitational forces and air resistance.

The students may have difficulty with the concept of gravity being the only force acting upon an upward-moving projectile. They often think that, since the object moves upward, it must be experiencing an upward force. The following system uses a short blast of air to launch a projectile – there is only an initial push and no thrust thereafter.

Practical activity

Pneumatic launch system

Launcher

Apparatus

The equipment shown in Figure 9.4 can be obtained from a plumbing agent/DIY store. We recommend a push-fit system, such as John Guest (Speedfit).

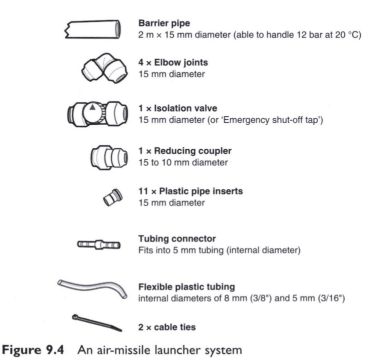

Barrier pipe
2 m × 15 mm diameter (able to handle 12 bar at 20 °C)

4 × Elbow joints
15 mm diameter

1 × Isolation valve
15 mm diameter (or 'Emergency shut-off tap')

1 × Reducing coupler
15 to 10 mm diameter

11 × Plastic pipe inserts
15 mm diameter

Tubing connector
Fits into 5 mm tubing (internal diameter)

Flexible plastic tubing
internal diameters of 8 mm (3/8") and 5 mm (3/16")

2 × cable ties

Figure 9.4   An air-missile launcher system

Construction

Cut the barrier pipe into five separate lengths: 3×45 cm, 2×10 cm, 1×35 cm. Ensure that burrs and sharp edges are removed if necessary with sand paper or emery cloth. With the exception of the free-end identified below, add a pipe insert into each end of the separate lengths of pipe. The inserts have a rubber 'O' ring which helps provide a secondary air-tight seal. Attach each of the pipes, elbow joints, isolation switch and reducer sections in the order shown in Figure 9.5.

The reducer section needs to be connected in an air-tight manner to the flexible tubing. Push the tubing and 'O' rings into the body of the reducer and tighten the plastic nut to lock the assembly in place. Insert the plastic tubing connector into one end of the 5 mm tubing. Carefully push both tubing and connector a short way into the free end of the 8 mm tubing. Use two cable ties on either side of the connector to create an air-tight seal (see Figure 9.6).

The pneumatic launch system is now ready to test. Turn the isolation switch to stop air from escaping out of the free end. Attach a foot or hand pump to the 5 mm tubing and introduce some air into the system – go no higher than 300 kPa (3 bar or 44 psi). Listen for air escaping – most likely at the reducer joint or where the two lengths of flexible tubing are connected.

Quickly turn the isolation switch to open the valve. Listen for a short burst of air from the free end: the faster the opening of the valve, the better the blast! The pipe system can usually cope well with pressures around 500 kPa (5 bar), but at higher pressures the links involving the flexible tubing might fail.

Air missile

The next step is to create an air missile for use with the pneumatic launcher. Once prepared, carefully push the missile on to the launch pipe. Ensure that it moves smoothly along the pipe and is far enough down so that the Plasticine works as a bung.

Apparatus

To make the air missile you will need the following equipment:

- One missile-fin template (see Figure 9.7)
- One rectangle of paper (A4 or A5)
- A 20 cm length of pipe (15 mm diameter)
- Adhesive tape and glue
- A lump of Plasticine

(Continued)

(Continued)

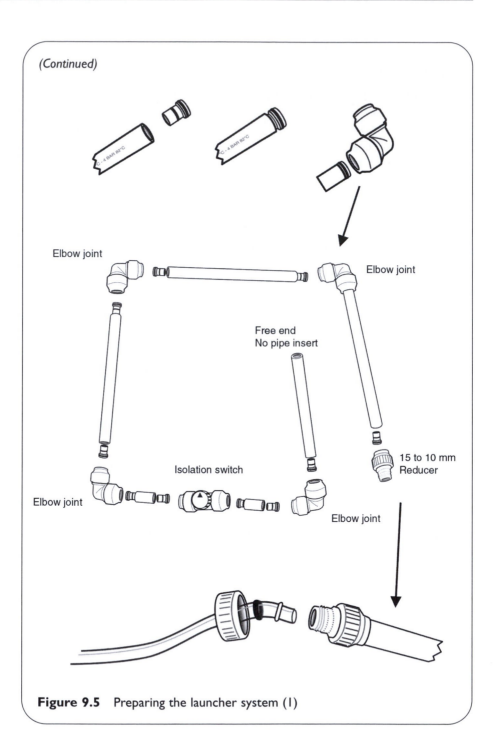

Figure 9.5   Preparing the launcher system (1)

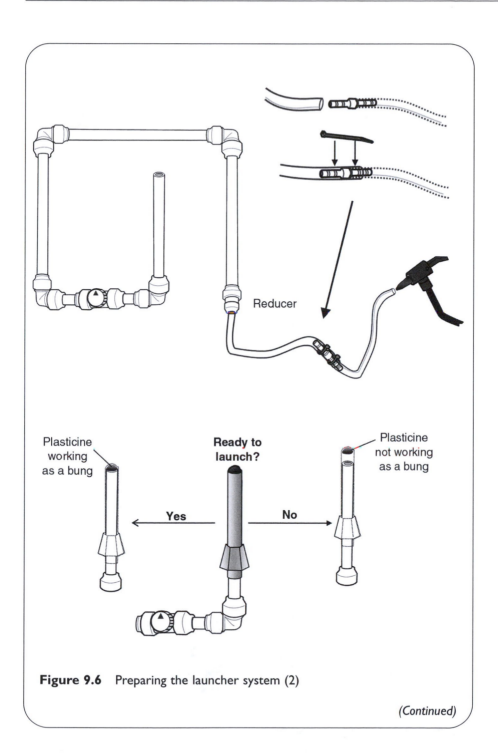

Figure 9.6 Preparing the launcher system (2)

(Continued)

(Continued)

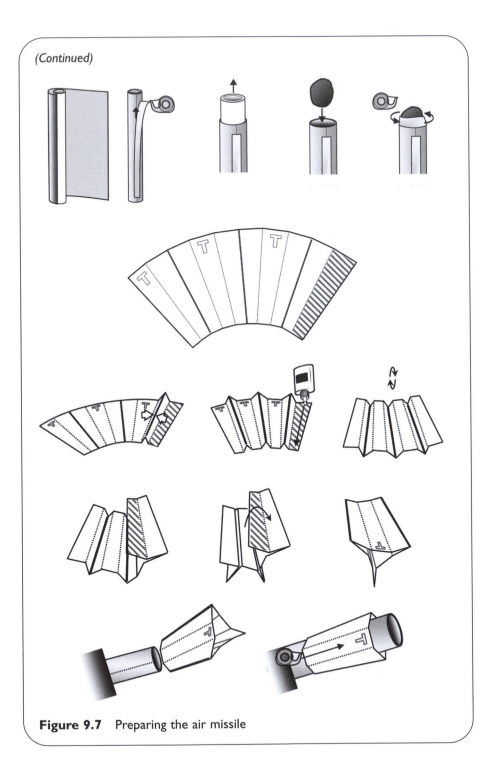

Figure 9.7   Preparing the air missile

Method

Roll the paper around the pipe. Ensure a tight fit, but not too tight. Use adhesive tape to hold the paper tube together. Push the pipe out of the tube and insert the lump of Plasticine into the top of the tube. Add tape to keep the lump fixed firmly in place.

Create a copy of the fin template. This has three bold lines. Pinch and fold the template along these lines so that they form three 'peaks'. Add glue to the shaded area on the template. Turn the template over so that the glued edge is on the underside. Fold over the glued edge. Bring it together with the opposite edge to form a cylinder with a triangular cross-section.

Push the free end of the paper tube through this cylinder. Push this far enough through to leave some of the tube sticking up beyond the fins. Add tape to fix the fins in place.

The launch pipe can be positioned to give several launch angles. Together with different pressures, your classes can investigate a variety of trajectories. There are two measurements that can be taken quickly and then used to analyse the missile's motion:

- Horizontal distance covered (m).
- Time of flight, from launch to landing (s).

Results from the missile launcher

Let's consider a hypothetical vertical launch under the influence of gravity (without air resistance). The missile moves off with an initial velocity, u (ms^{-1}). After a time of t (s) the missile moves a short distance s (m) upward but the velocity has reduced to v (ms^{-1}) (see Figure 9.8).

Over the time period (t seconds) we know the starting and finishing velocities and so can generate a velocity–time chart (see Figure 9.8):

- The graph shows steady (uniform) change in velocity. The gradient equals the acceleration, a (ms^{-2}).
- The area under the velocity–time graph represents the distance travelled by the missile. We can consider the area to comprise two regular shapes – a rectangle and a triangle – and with some simple geometry we can determine a value for s (m).

We can now combine the equations shown in Figure 9.8. The resulting equation is one of a number of the standard equations of motion that is commonly reduced to:

$$s = vt - \tfrac{1}{2}at^2$$

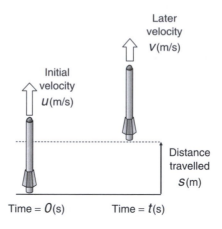

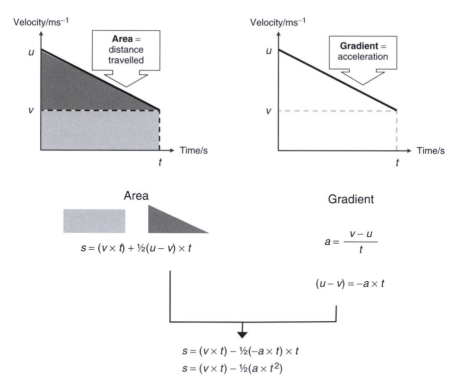

Figure 9.8 Time–distance and time–velocity charts

Example analysis

A rocket is launched using a pressure of 3 bar. The launch angle was not recorded but the missile covered 45 m (horizontal distance) in 3·4 seconds.

We can break the trajectory up into horizontal (v_x, s_x) and vertical components (v_y, s_y).

Let's consider just the horizontal components (ignoring air resistance):

$$\text{Average velocity, } v_x \quad = s_x \div t$$
$$= 45 \div 3.4$$
$$= 13.2 \text{ ms}^{-1}$$

As the rocket moves upwards, its vertical velocity decelerates under gravity. As it flies up the missile reaches a maximum height – the apex of its trajectory. At this point its vertical velocity, v_y, equals zero. This occurs when the time, t, equals half the total time of flight.

The following equation of motion:

$$s = vt - \tfrac{1}{2}at^2$$

reduces to:

$$s = -\tfrac{1}{2}at^2$$

During the 3.4 seconds of flight, the apex will be reached in half this time (1.7 s). At this point, $v_y = 0$:

$$\text{Height reached, } s_y \quad = v_y t - \tfrac{1}{2}at^2$$
$$= 0 - \tfrac{1}{2}at^2$$
$$= -\tfrac{1}{2} \times -9.81 \times (1.7)^2$$
$$= 14.2 \text{ m}$$

Once the rocket lands, it will have travelled equal vertical distances or displacement up (+direction) and then down (–direction). Overall these measurements cancel to give a total displacement of zero (consider if you shoot a missile straight up – it should land where it started from!):

$$\text{Total distance, } s_y \quad = v_y t - \tfrac{1}{2}at^2$$
$$= 0 \text{ m}$$

Therefore:

$$v_y t = \tfrac{1}{2}at^2$$
$$v_y = \tfrac{1}{2}at$$
$$= \tfrac{1}{2} \times -9.81 \times 3.4$$
$$= -16.7 \text{ ms}^{-1}$$

The same result can be obtained by considering the missile as a falling body – dropping from its apex under gravity. We can use the equation to calculate the velocity reached as the missile falls 14.18 m to the ground. Velocity of a body falling from rest (zero drag):

$$v = \sqrt{(2 \times a \times s)} \text{ ms}^{-1}$$

$$v_y = \sqrt{2as}$$
$$= \sqrt{(2 \times 9.81 \times 14.18)}$$
$$= 16.7 \text{ ms}^{-1}$$

Further reading

Inexpensive (and free) software capable of frame-by-frame viewing is available for downloading. This includes the following:

www.hk-phy.org/mvas/
   Motion Video Analysis Software.

www.lsw.com/videopoint/
   Videopoint.

www.learninginmotion.com/products/measurement/index.html
   Measurement in Motion.

www.physicstoolkit.com/
   Physics Toolkit – formerly World-in-Motion.

www3.science.tamu.edu/cmse/videoanalysis/
   A website that contains short video clips that can be used for teaching physics.

Section 4

The Earth and its place in the universe

In this section, of three chapters, you will be introduced to the science of:

- earthquakes and volcanoes;
- stars and their evolution;
- the solar system; and
- global warming and its interpretation.

This links to, and will help you deliver, the various national curricula for England, Ireland, Scotland and Wales as set out below.

By working through this section it is expected that you will be able to describe and explain:

- how volcanoes and earthquakes occur;
- the formation and evolution of stars;
- ideas behind constellations; and
- the science and controversy surrounding global warming.

Please turn over to see how this section relates to your curriculum.

National Curriculum for England	Junior Certificate Science Syllabus	Environmental Studies – Society, Science and Technology	Science in the National Curriculum for Wales
KS3, 3.4a Geological activity is caused by chemical and physical processes **b** Astronomy and space science provide insight into the nature and observed motions of the sun, moon, stars, planets and other celestial bodies **KS4, 8** The surface and the atmosphere of the Earth have changed since the Earth's origin and are changing at present **c** The solar system is part of the universe, which has changed since its origin and continues to show long-term changes		Earth in space: Developing an understanding of the position of the Earth in the solar system and the universe, and the effects of its movement and that of the Moon	**KS3, 1** That the oribital time for a planet/satellite depends on its distance from the Sun/Earth, and that this movement is determined by gravitational force **4** That the Sun and other stars are light sources and that planets and other bodies are seen by scattered light **KS4, 4.3** How stars evolve over a long time-scale **4** About some ideas used to explain the evolution of the universe into its present state

10 The Earth, earthquakes and volcanoes

Ruth Richards

This chapter covers:

- the rock cycle
- the Earth's structure (crust, mantle and core)
- earthquakes
- plate tectonics
- volcanoes.

 ## Test your own knowledge

Before reading the material in this chapter test your current knowledge with the following questions:

1. What is the rock cycle?
2. What are the three main types of rocks and how do they form?
3. How long does it take for rocks to form? Are some rocks formed faster than others? Can you give any examples of types of rocks that form slowly and others that form quickly?
4. Why do earthquakes happen?
5. What is a) a mineral; and b) a rock?

Most teachers would struggle with the last question, let alone the students. Of course, once you know the answer it's obvious:

- **Mineral**: An arrangement of atoms involving specific elements only. For example, quartz is SiO_2 – one Si atom to every two O atoms. Calcite is $CaCO_3$ – one Ca atom, one C atom and three O atoms. Most other mineral compositions are too complex for GCSE level.

- **Rock**: A collection of minerals in a solid form. The exact minerals involved depend on how they are formed. These may be sedimentary, igneous or metamorphic.

The topics in this chapter are based on everyday ideas and items. The geological demonstrations and activities are very cheap, involving the use of everyday food or non-food items to illustrate ideas simply. The focus of this chapter is on the practical aspects rather than on the deep theory (see the Further reading section at the end of the chapter for a suggested theoretical text).

Fundamentals of the Earth: the rock cycle

It is impossible to understand how earthquakes and volcanoes operate without considering the rock cycle. Take a look at the rock cycle and ensure that you understand how the processes relate to the separate rock types. For example, weathering and erosion yield fragments of rock that form sediments. These sediments are transported by water in streams and rivers, deposited, and eventually formed into a sedimentary rock. The actual change of sediment into solid rock is called 'lithification'. In this example the processes involved are erosion, weathering, transport, deposition and lithification.

A diagram of the rock cycle is often used to explain the concept by linking the processes together. These diagrams are commonly available. This is a good approach, but it makes the Earth seem fairly static, which of course it is not. The main problem is that the processes usually happen so slowly it is difficult to see how one rock transforms into another rock. Why does a sedimentary rock become a metamorphic or igneous one? The answer is all tied up with plate tectonics which, of course, link to our ideas about earthquakes.

Practical activity

Looking at specimens

What about teaching geology in a practical way? We would always advocate the use of hand specimens, but you may not have access to a good collection yourself. It is worth investing in a few hand specimens, such as those suggested in Table 10.1.

Table 10.1   *Hand specimens*

Rock/mineral category	Suggested specimens
Sedimentary	Shelly limestone
	Oolitic limestone
	Sandstone
	Conglomerate
	Shale
Igneous	Peridotite
	Gabbro
	Basalt
	Shap granite
	Rhyolite
	Pumice
	Obsidian
Metamorphic	Gneiss
	Schist
	Slate
	Marble
Minerals	Calcite
	Quartz
	Olivine
	Haematite
	Galena
	Iron pyrites

Alternatively, rocks are used everywhere, such as the frontages on buildings and as head stones in graveyards. A survey of your school may yield interesting specimens to study, and a visit to the local high street or graveyard could yield others. It is worth bearing in mind that, if you do not have access to good specimens, this may make an interesting and more memorable way of teaching the basics.

The Earth's structure

The Earth is made of layers that have different compositions and properties. The three main layers are the crust, mantle and core. Scientists have subdivided these layers further. There is the continental and oceanic crust; the upper and lower mantle; and the inner and outer core.

Practical activity

The Earth's structure

A simple way of illustrating the Earth's structure is by using a cream egg or a similar confectionary item. The yolk shows the core – a part which is significantly bigger than most people envisage. The white is the mantle and the chocolate is the crust. Alternatively, the students could create a scale model of the Earth's structure, marking the distance from each boundary to the centre of the Earth. This could then be displayed in the classroom.

How do we know that this is the structure of the Earth? Do we just take this at face value? What evidence is there to tell us this? The first way to establish that the rocks under the surface are different from those at depth is to look at the density of the rocks found at the surface (2.9 g/cm³) and to see how this compares with the calculated average for the whole Earth (5.5 g/cm³). The values are very different, suggesting more dense rocks at depth.

Practical activity

Calculating the density of rocks

Fill a displacement (eureka) can with water. Ensure the dripping has stopped before commencing the activity. Measure the mass of a rock specimen that can fit into the can, to two decimal places. Place the specimen carefully into the displacement can making sure there is no splashing.

Collect all the water that is displaced in a measuring cylinder, remembering to wait for the water to stop dripping. Calculate the density by using the following equation:

$$\text{Density (g/cm}^3) = \frac{\text{Mass of rock (g)}}{\text{Volume of water (cm}^3)}$$

This works best if you calculate the density of sandstone, granite, gabbro and peridotite. The peridotite should yield the highest value. This is because it is composed almost entirely of a mineral called olivine which is rich in iron and magnesium. The least dense rock should be the sandstone.

Other evidence for the Earth's structure is both direct and indirect – things we can see and things that we can infer, as summarized in Table 10.2.

Table 10.2   *Evidence for the Earth's structure*

Evidence	Explanation
Direct	
Overturned oceanic crust (ophiolite)	Fragments of crust have been overturned during plate movements, exposing around 7 km of igneous rocks. The lowest rock type (peridotite) is rarely seen at the surface and probably represents the composition of the upper part of the mantle. There are examples of these in the Troodos Mountains in Cyprus, and in the Lizard in Cornwall
Volcanic products (xenoliths)	Volcanoes bringing up rocks from further down in the crust which are not normally associated with the volcano. These solid fragments are of a different composition and a higher density, again rarely seen at the surface. This suggests a different composition at depth. These are called mantle xenoliths
Evidence from mines and boreholes	Deep mines notice an increase in temperature at depth. This is called the geothermal gradient, which is around 25 °/km
Indirect	
Meteorites	Meteorites are thought to be the fragmented remains or debris left over from the formation of the solar system and thus their composition probably mirrors that of the Earth. The composition of meteorites may be very dense and metallic (approximately 8 g/cm^3) or less dense and stony (approximately 3.5 g/cm^3). This is thought to reflect the composition of the core and mantle
Earthquakes	Earthquake waves increase in velocity as they pass through the Earth and are refracted. These changes signify changes in the composition, properties and density of the rocks. It must be stressed that earthquake waves slow down with increasing density: they do not speed up. They become faster the more incompressible and rigid the rocks become. There are two main types of earthquake waves to consider, P and S waves. It is known that S waves cannot pass through liquids. The passage of S waves stops at the core mantle boundary, suggesting the outer core is molten
The Earth's magnetic field	The Earth behaves like a giant bar magnet. The magnetic field is believed to be caused by the dynamo effect of moving molten material in the outer core. If the core was completely solid the Earth would not have a magnetic field

Practical activity

The Earth's magnetic field

You can demonstrate the Earth's magnetic field by using a simple bar magnet, a piece of paper placed on top of this and iron filings sprinkled on top of the paper. The resultant pattern of magnetism is similar to that of the Earth (see Figure 10.1).

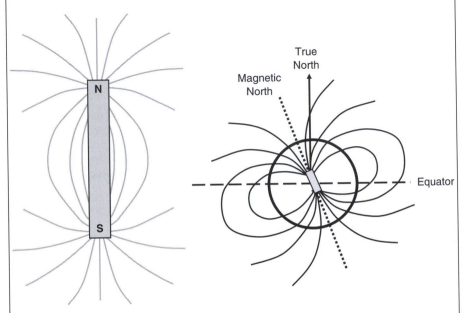

Figure 10.1   Magnetic field generated in a bar magnet and a model of the Earth's magnetic field

The crust

The Earth's surface is covered with two types of crust: continental and oceanic. The oceanic crust is thinner and denser than the continental crust. It also represents the youngest crust geologically.

Oceanic crust is formed at mid-ocean ridges or spreading centres, and it has a density of around 2.9 g/cm³. The spreading ridges are one piece of evidence for the plate tectonic model of crustal movement (see later in this chapter). The continental crust has an increased amount of less dense minerals (a density of around 2.7 g/cm³), meaning they contain a great deal of SiO_2.

The difference in density means that the more dense oceanic crust will sink below the less dense continental crust, as they do at convergent (destructive) plate boundaries. Some continental crust is geologically very old and forms, in some parts of the world such as Africa and Antarctica, old, stable crust known as cratons.

The lithosphere is a complicated term used in some specifications. This is not simply another name for the crust! It represents the crust and the uppermost part of the mantle. The uppermost part of the mantle is cool enough for it to remain solid, and it behaves in a brittle way, rather like the crust. Other parts of the mantle below the lithosphere behave in a semi-plastic way, rather like thick syrup.

The mantle

The top of the upper mantle is rigid and brittle and it behaves the same way as the crust that is on top of it. Below this is a zone called the low-velocity layer, where the speed of both P and S waves slows down. This suggests that it is in fact partially melted rather than being a liquid.

This can be explained using a chocolate-chip cookie or a muffin. Placing either of these in a microwave will result in the chocolate being molten and the rest of the item solid. This is a good analogy for what happens in this part of the mantle: this part will flow, very, very slowly.

The composition of the upper mantle is thought to be peridotite. The lower mantle is a solid because S waves can pass through it, and it is thought to be of the same composition as the upper mantle and to mirror the composition of stony meteorites.

The core

This is divided into the inner and outer core. The inner core is thought to be solid and made of iron and nickel. The outer core is believed to be iron and nickel, but in a liquid phase. This allows movements or currents to occur within it to generate the Earth's magnetic field. The P waves slow down at the outer core boundary, suggesting that it is less rigid and more compressible than the lower mantle. S waves can pass through the solid core. Where do these come from, if they cannot pass through the outer core? These S waves are, in fact, generated at the inner/outer core boundary. The calculated density of the core is variable, at around 14 g/cm^3. This is significantly higher than the average whole-Earth density at 5.5 g/cm^3.

Earthquakes

The main evidence for the Earth's structure is derived from the earthquake waves that pass through the Earth. The changes in the behaviour of these earthquake waves reflect the changes in composition and state at depth. Earthquake waves speed up as the rocks at depth become more incompressible and rigid. The density also increases but, as stated previously, this slows down the passage of earthquake waves. So the changes in incompressibility and rigidity must increase faster with depth than density.

So what is an earthquake? What does it actually represent? Generally, earthquakes are associated with plate movements or faulting. Quite a lot of movement along a fault will occur without being noticed, as it happens fairly continually. If something prevents this movement, then there is a build-up of pressure which is all released in one go, because there is movement along the fault. An analogy is an elastic band. If you stretch an elastic band it will gradually change shape until, snap, it returns to its original shape. The longer there is between earthquakes, the more energy is stored up, the more pressure there is, the more devastating the earthquake because there is more energy to be released. This is called the seismic gap theory. This time gap between each earthquake can often be a predictor as to when the next one will happen. A large earthquake is therefore due in San Francisco imminently.

How science works

Tsunamis are waves that are generated by the displacement of a large volume of water, as a result of a fault movement or earthquake. They are often erroneously called 'tidal waves' but have nothing to do with tides. Most earthquakes are not followed by a tsunami but, as earthquake waves travel quickly, there may be several hours' warning of such a disaster.

The Indian Ocean Tsunami Warning System was established by UNESCO after around 250,000 people died following the earthquake near Banda Aceh (Sumatra) in 2004. Prior to this there was no co-ordinated warning system in the Indian Ocean, which could have saved thousands of lives.

Practical activity

Liquefaction

Liquefaction occurs when there is separation of particles and water underground. This can be illustrated easily by using a beaker full of sand and Lego houses. Alternatively, rubber bungs work very well.

Add water to the beaker so that the sand is fairly saturated and then tap the bench next to the beaker. The houses will sink and fall over in the sand. The more water, the quicker this process occurs.

How science works

Most people who die as a result of an earthquake do not die as a result of the earthquake itself, but due to the poor standard of the buildings and their not being 'earthquake proof'. They may also die as a result of the onset of disease afterwards, usually caused by a lack of fresh water.

In 1985, Mexico City was hit by a large earthquake. The city itself had been built on an old lake bed, which meant that the sediments were unconsolidated (not stuck together to form rock). As the earthquake progressed, liquefaction occurred, meaning that many buildings collapsed that should have withstood the earthquake.

Constructing a building on poor foundations or without flexible foundations in an earthquake zone will only have devastating effects. There have been massive advancements in earthquake proofing buildings in earthquake zones, and even the production of earthquake-proof wallpaper!

Plate tectonics

The Earth is covered with a series of plates, of many different sizes and shapes. These are moving slowly – the sort of speed your finger nail grows. The areas where the plates meet are called plate margins, and these can be located easily by looking at some familiar features: earthquake zones, chains of volcanoes, mountain chains, oceanic trenches and rift valleys. It is the plate boundaries that are important because this is where 'things' happen.

Plate boundaries may be divergent (constructive) or convergent (destructive). A summary is shown in Table 10.3 and in Figure 10.2.

Table 10.3   *Plate boundaries*

Type of boundary	Example	Explanation
Divergent	Mid-oceanic ridges (Mid-Atlantic Ridge)	Magma rises in the mantle because it has been heated. Magma is less dense than surroundings and the crust is forced apart, allowing eruptions of basalt

(Continued)

Table 10.3 *(Continued)*

Type of boundary	Example	Explanation
Convergent	1. Continental–oceanic (Andes)	More dense oceanic crust collides with less dense continental crust. The dense crust sinks beneath less dense, melts and then rises again to form a magma chamber in a mountain chain. This fuels eruptions
	2. Continental–continental (Himalayas)	Collision of continents to form mountain ranges
	3. Oceanic–oceanic (Japan)	One plate sinks below the other, forming mountain chains which stick out of the ocean as an island arc system

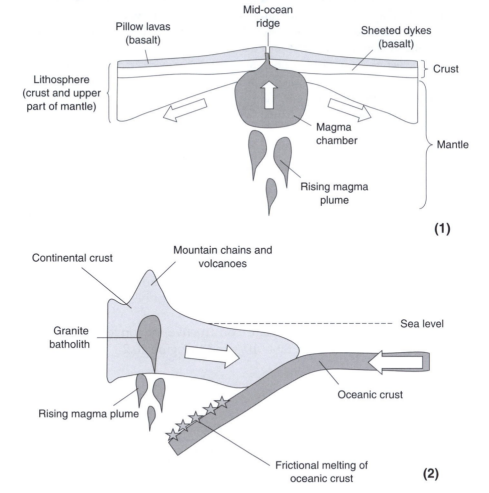

Figure 10.2 Divergent and convergent plate boundaries

1. Divergent plate boundary (Mid-Oceanic Ridge). Arrows show the direction of mantle convection
2. Convergent plate boundary (oceanic–continental). Arrows show the direction of plate movement

Practical activity

Plate tectonic jigsaw

Find a map of the world with an outline of the continents and with the plates visible (some good ones are available on the US Geological Survey website – see the 'Further reading' section at the end of this chapter). Cut out the plates along the plate boundaries. Stick these on another piece of paper. You have now prepared a plate jigsaw for your class to cut out and stick back together.

Continental drift versus plate tectonics – these are terms that are often used interchangeably. This should not be the case. Continental drift is the movement apart of the continents, but is without a scientific explanation. This drift was first described in 1912 by Alfred Wegener, when it was noticed that the continents of South America and Africa showed a 'jigsaw fit'.

Plate tectonics is the theory that puts forward a mechanism for the movement of the continents. This was described much later in the 1960s, when Arthur Holmes proposed a conveyer-belt system for the movement of the continents. This was taken further in 1962 when Harry Hess proposed that new ocean floor was being created at mid-ocean ridges and consumed at ocean trenches.

How science works

Ideas about plate tectonics were aided greatly during the Second World War. This was because the ocean floor was mapped to provide a tactical advantage for submarines. The mapping revealed huge mountain chains running down the centre of the oceans. It was as a result of this mapping that the term 'sea-floor spreading' was coined.

Practical activity

Convection model

Convection can be illustrated by using potassium permanganate as a dye. Embed a large crystal into a lump of Vaseline. Stick this carefully to the bottom of a 1 litre beaker and fill with water (see Figure 10.3). Gentle heating directly under the Vaseline will cause it to melt. The dye then streams up through the water, allowing convection cells to be picked out. This happens very quickly and, very soon, the whole beaker is full of purple water.

(Continued)

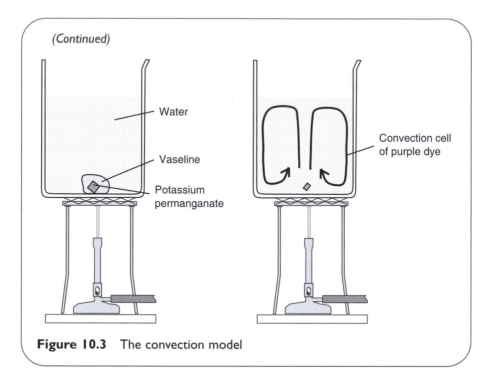

Figure 10.3 The convection model

The water closest to the Bunsen flame heats up more quickly and expands. As it does this it becomes less dense and rises, fuelling the convection in the beaker. It subsequently cools down and sinks at the edges of the beaker. This is what happens in the mantle, and the source of heat is radioactive decay in the core.

Practical activity

Illustrating plate tectonics

Take a 1 litre beaker and pour in syrup to a depth of at least 7cm. Take a digestive biscuit and break into several large and some smaller pieces. Reassemble these pieces into a whole biscuit and place in the centre of the beaker on top of the syrup.

Heating the syrup sets up convection currents. This will allow the pieces of biscuit to separate because the fragments are suspended on the top of the syrup. They are literally dragged apart.

Volcanoes

Why do volcanoes appear where they are? Is there a pattern? The answer is yes, there is a pattern. Volcanoes appear where there is subducting crust along plate margins or heating of the crust close to the surface. This may be the continental–oceanic crustal boundary where oceanic crust is being subducted and melted under the continental crust. This is mainly due to frictional heat, as the oceanic crust is rubbed along the base of the continental crust. This produces pockets of less dense molten material, which rises up into the continental crust and in some cases erupts at the surface. A good example of this type of margin is the Cascade Mountains in North America. The most famous eruption here was, of course, Mount St Helens in 1980.

Volcanoes also occur at an oceanic–oceanic boundary, where there is a formation of small islands in a row, as with Japan. This is known as an island arc system.

Hot spots are more elusive. These occur where part of the oceanic crust has a plume of hot mantle material rising below it. This causes an island to form at the surface. If the plate is moving, the hot spot does not, and this can form a chain of islands, such as the Hawaiian Islands.

So volcanoes are directly linked to plate tectonics. As these plate margins have faults and crustal movements, they also appear in the same place as earthquakes. If you plot the position of the largest earthquakes and volcanoes on a world map, you will see there is a correlation between where these occur. The Pacific 'ring of fire' is an example of this.

Large v. small crystals in a rock

In igneous rocks, why are some crystals small and some large? It is all to do with collision theory. In a melt (magma), one element will combine with another if they collide with enough energy for a bond to form between them. The longer the melt is in a liquid state, the more collisions occur. The more successful collisions, the more elements are correctly added to the size of a growing crystal. Only collisions between the correct elements will result in the growth of the crystal.

This becomes even more complicated because different minerals become stable at different temperatures. For example, plagioclase feldspar becomes stable (crystallizes) at a higher temperature than quartz or biotite mica. These are three common minerals found in granite. This is an important concept at advanced level and beyond and is known as Bowen's Reaction Series. This means that, at some point, you will have crystals and liquid together, rather like a slush-puppy drink. This also explains why some crystals in the same rock are larger than others.

Many specifications stipulate the use of certain rocks to illustrate changes in crystal size. Table 10.4 offers some suggestions.

It should be noted that all the rocks low in silica are generally dark in colour. Rocks high in silica are generally light in colour, with the exception of obsidian, which is black.

Table 10.4   *Rocks to illustrate changes in crystal size*

		Cooling rate		
		Supercooled or glassy	Fast	Slow
Suggested rock type	Low in silica	Pitchstone	Basalt	Gabbro
	High in silica	Obsidian	Rhyolite	Granite

Pumice is also an example of a supercooled rock, but this contains many bubbles of gas which makes its formation much harder to explain. Pumice is formed as it is ejected out of a volcanic vent. As it is ejected, the fluids turn from a liquid to a gaseous state because there is a decrease in pressure. This can be illustrated by removing the cap from a fizzy drinks bottle and seeing many bubbles of gas appear. The release of pressure allows the gas bubbles to be released. Pumice is the only rock that can float on water.

Practical activity

Crystal formation

How cooling rates can affect the size of crystal growth can easily be illustrated using a Crunchie or similar confectionary item. The size of the bubbles equals the size of the crystals. The centre has much larger bubbles because it has cooled much more slowly. The supercooled extremities only allow bubbles of a much smaller size to form. This matches exactly what we see in small intrusions, such as dykes or sills. (Sills are intrusions parallel with sedimentary bedding, while dykes cut through them.)

Practical activity

Cooling lava or magma

Large intrusions will cool more slowly than small ones. This can be illustrated using different-sized tin cans or containers which are filled with hot water and allowed to cool. Temperature changes can be noted using a simple thermometer or by a data logger fitted with a temperature probe. Stearic acid can be employed as an alternative, using two differently sized tubes (e.g. a boiling tube and a test tube) as a comparison.

The cooling curves constructed from these data help to explain why crystal size is smallest at the edges of a large intrusion (chilled margins) or throughout minor intrusions because the heat radiates away quickly. Large crystals found in coarse crystalline rocks, such as granite, have cooled more slowly and at depth where the heat cannot escape as easily (well insulated).

Engaging activities

The following practical ideas are rather messy but they allow the students to access in a practical way some rather big concepts about the formation of rocks.

Making a volcano

This is a simple model that is fun to make and 'erupt'. It can be constructed using damp sand piled up into a cone shape with a hole placed in its centre. Adding bicarbonate of soda to the centre is the starting point. You can mix the bicarbonate of soda with powdered paint. Try one colour at the bottom and one at the top. Food dye can be used as an alternative. Pour acetic acid (vinegar) into the hole and stand back to watch your volcano erupt. If you have used two colours, you will see the early eruption in one colour and the late eruption in another.

Crystal formation

An alternative and much more exciting way of illustrating crystal formation and cooling rates is by making your own cinder toffee in class, as a demonstration. Try the following the following recipe:

- 200 g caster sugar
- Three are four tablespoons of syrup
- One or two tablespoons of water
- One tablespoon bicarbonate of soda

Make sure you add water to reduce the sugar's melting temperature. Also be careful not to burn the sugar. If this happens, it will go very dark brown and will smell dreadful.

Heat the sugar, syrup and water in a pan until gently bubbling. Watch very carefully as it will change colour and become darker. This will take about five

(Continued)

(Continued)

minutes in total. Add the bicarbonate of soda and, using a bomb whisk, beat until it starts to increase in volume. This will happen within seconds, so beware! Turn out on to a suitable surface, such as aluminium foil, and leave to cool.

If you provide your own pan and utensils from home, you could distribute pieces to the students at the end of the lesson, if appropriate.

Beware, also that the volume of the mixture will increase dramatically in size. It will even continue to 'grow' after you have poured it out to cool down. It should be cool and hard in 30 minutes.

Further reading

Armstrong, D., Mugglestone, F., Richards, R. and Stratton, F. (2008) *OCR Geology*. Harlow: Pearson Education.
An excellent summary of the geological knowledge required at A-level and a good starting point for those wanting to improve their geological knowledge.

www.qca.org.uk/qca_9437.aspx
The QCA How Science Works website.

http://vulcan.wr.usgs.gov/Glossary/PlateTectonics/Graphics/framework. html
The US Geological Survey website where maps and graphics of active volcanoes, plate tectonics, hot spots, 'rings of fire', etc., can be found.

11 Heavens above: stars and planets

Gren Ireson

This chapter covers:

- the life of a star
- nuclear synthesis
- solar systems
- galaxies
- light years
- constellations
- the fate of the universe.

 Test your own knowledge

Before reading the material in this chapter test your current knowledge with the following questions:

1. What is a solar system?
2. Our solar system is made up of eight planets. What are they and can you place then in order of distance from the Sun?
3. When people talk about satellites they generally mean *artificial* ones. What is the name of the Earth's only *natural* satellite?
4. How long does it take light to reach the Earth from a) the Sun; and b) the Moon?
5. What is the name of our nearest star?

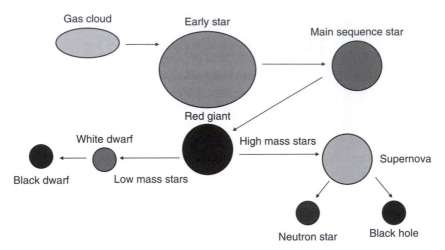

Figure 11.1   The life cycle of a star

Star basics

A star radiates light and heat and other electromagnetic radiation (see Chapter 7). The life of a star can be summarized simply as shown in Figure 11.1. The accepted scientific reasoning for the development of a star, and the entire universe, is the 'big bang'. About 13.7 billion years ago all the matter and energy in the universe exploded and started to expand. As things cooled down, matter started to form and gravity took over. The following stages were set in motion:

- Gravitational attraction brings together the material in the cloud of gas and dust.
- The early star becomes hot enough for the process of nuclear synthesis – building more massive elements from lighter ones – to start. This star is now known as a 'main sequence' star, where the outward force due to the radiation is matched with the inward force due to gravitational attraction. Main sequence stars are stable for many billions of years.
- The 'fuel' in the star eventually runs out and, following a period of expansion, the star (called a red giant) develops in one of two ways, depending on its mass.
- *Light* stars, like our sun, cool and contract, becoming first a white dwarf and finally a black dwarf emitting no more light.
- *Massive* stars undergo a series of expansions and contractions, building up more massive elements before they eventually tear themselves apart in a supernova, leaving a very dense core.
- The remaining dense core becomes a neutron star or, if it is dense enough, a black hole.

The material thrown out during the supernova is 'recycled' in new clouds of dust and gas to start the process over again, so everything in the universe, even us, can be said to be made of star dust.

Nuclear synthesis

In a star, temperature and pressure are so high that, for example, hydrogen nuclei can fuse together eventually to form helium nuclei:

$${}^1_1H + {}^1_1H \rightarrow {}^2_1H + e^+ + v \text{ where } e^+ \text{ is a positron and v a neutrino}$$

$${}^1_1H + {}^2_1H \rightarrow {}^3_2He + v$$

$${}^3_2He + {}^3_2He \rightarrow {}^4_2He + {}^1_1H + {}^1_1H$$

This process can be thought of as a simple input–output mechanism, as follows:

$6 \times {}^1_1H$ input giving ${}^4_2He + 2 \times e^+ + 2 \times v + 2 \times {}^1_1H$ output, which simplifies to:

$4 \times {}^1_1H$ input giving ${}^4_2He + 2 \times e' + 2 \times v$ output

The energy released is then calculated via the famous $\Delta E = \Delta mc^2$ – the change in *mass* multiplied by the *speed of light squared* gives the change in *energy* because the total mass of $4 \times {}^1_1H$ is more than the total mass of ${}^4_2He$.

Solar system

A solar system is a star that has planets orbiting. In our solar system the star is the Sun and the eight planets moving out from the Sun are Mercury, Venus, the Earth, Mars, Jupiter, Saturn, Uranus and Neptune. Until 2006 we had an additional planet, Pluto, in our solar system. Pluto sits beyond Neptune in its orbit but the International Astronomical Union (IAU) reclassified it as a dwarf planet. The IAU set three criteria for a planet:

- It is in orbit around a sun.
- It has sufficient mass to form itself into a sphere (hydrostatic equilibrium).
- It dominates its orbit – i.e. there is nothing else of comparable mass in the same orbit region.

Pluto fails on this final count and so, following its discovery in 1930, it lost its planetary status just 76 years later.

Table 11.1 *Moons as of 2008*

Planet	Number of moons	Examples
Mercury	0	
Venus	0	
Earth	1	Moon
Mars	2	Deimos, Phobos
Jupiter	63	Adrastea, Callisto
Saturn	60	Dione, Atlas
Uranus	27	Ariel, Desdemona
Neptune	13	Triton, Larissa

Planets may also have other bodies, natural and artificial, orbiting them. The most obvious of these are our Moon and satellites giving us weather information and television channels. In fact all bodies orbiting a planet are known as satellites, but natural satellites are usually known as moons. It is not just the Earth that as a moon, as Table 11.1 indicates.

In order to help remember the order of the planets in terms of distance from the Sun, you can use a mnemonic: My, Very, Easy, Method, Just, Speeds, Up (the), Naming. This works for me, but can you think of your own?

The length of time it takes a planet to orbit the Sun is its year. Planets also spin on their axis, and the time for one complete revolution is the planet's day. The length of the year and day varies greatly from planet to planet, as shown in Table 11.2.

Table 11.2 *Days and years of the planets*

Planet	Day (in Earth days)	Year (in Earth days)
Mercury	59.00	88.00
Venus	243.00	225.00
Earth	1.00	365.25
Mars	1.02	687.00
Jupiter	0.42	4380.00
Saturn	0.44	10 950.00
Uranus	0.63	30 660.00
Neptune	0.75	60 225.00

Beyond our solar system

Our solar system – the Sun and eight planets – is part of a galaxy. Our galaxy is called the Milky Way and it looks a little like a Catherine wheel with spiral arms (see Figure 11.2). Notice the dashed line. This is known as the Orion Arm and is where our solar system sits.

Figure 11.2 The milky way

Our galaxy is just one of billions in the universe, but the distances between them are almost unimaginable. A rule-of-thumb scale could be used here to say:

- Let a typical star (sun)–planet distance be 1 unit.
- Then a typical star–star distance in a galaxy would be 10 000 000 units.
- A typical galaxy–galaxy distance would then be 10 000 000 000 000 units.

Light years, days, minutes …

Because the distances involved are so huge, astronomers measure distance in light years (or days or minutes). A light year is simply the distance light would travel, through space, in one year.

Given that light travels through space at 300 000 000 ms^{-1} which, if you do the mathematics, gives a distance of:

$$1 \text{ year} = 31\ 557\ 600 \text{ seconds } (365.25 \times 24 \times 3\ 600)$$

$$31\ 557\ 600 \times 300\ 000\ 000 = 9\ 467\ 280\ 000\ 000\ 000 \text{ m}$$

One light year is equivalent to 9.47×10^{15} m.

Our Sun is approximately 150 000 000 km or 150 000 000 000 m from the Earth (this distance varies during the Earth's orbit since, as with all planets, the orbits are elliptical rather than circular). Using the light units we can say that the Sun is 500 light seconds or 8.3 light minutes away. It may seem odd but we only ever know what our Sun was like 8.3 minutes ago as it takes light that long to reach us.

After the Sun our next nearest star, Proxima Centauri, is an amazing 4.2 light years away. You could try to calculate this distance in metres.

Constellations

Constellations are really just something people have made up! Poets, artists and early navigators have all had a say. What a constellation does do, however, is make it easier for use to recognize which stars we are looking at. For example, if we consider the constellation Orion (see Figure 11.3), three bright stars in a line can be recognized as Orion's belt.

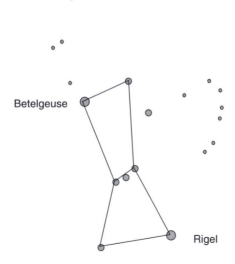

Figure 11.3   The Orion constellation

This then points to Betelgeuse (on his right shoulder) and Rigel (on his left knee). You may be wondering why on earth we talk about knees and shoulders but, when the constellations are named, people 'see' the shape within it – in this case, Orion the hunter. Your interpretation is probably as good as anyone else's, but Figure 11.4 gives the idea.

Where will it all end?

As stated earlier in this chapter, the accepted scientific theory is that the universe was created from the 'big bang' some 14 billion years ago and that it has been expanding ever since. While scientists are in general

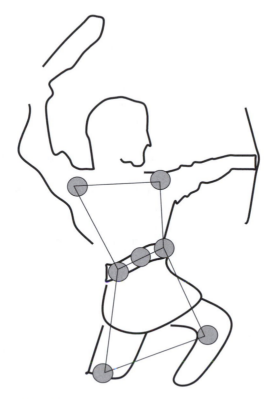

Figure 11.4 Imagining Orion

agreement over this, the fate of the universe is rather more open. It is thought that one of two outcomes could occur:

- The universe will expand for ever, with galaxies becoming ever more distant from each other.
- The force due to gravity will eventually halt the expansion and draw all the matter together, leading to a 'big crunch'.

However, in 1998 it was discovered that not only is the universe still expanding but also that the rate at which it is expanding is increasing. Because we do not know exactly what is causing the acceleration it is called 'dark energy' – we can't see it and we don't know what it is.

This new evidence is important since it opens up new possibilities. At present, solar systems and galaxies remain in tact – galaxies simply get further from each other. However, we can now consider that the dark energy may:

- eventually tear apart even galaxies and solar systems; or
- become dissipated and allow gravity to take over; or
- even become attractive.

How science works

Our understanding of the universe or even our solar system has developed only recently. The notion of the Earth orbiting the Sun rather than the Sun orbiting the Earth was of great concern to the church in Europe when Galileo Galilei argued for the former position between 1615 and 1632. He was found guilty of heresy and put under house arrest (for more about Galileo, see Chapter 9).

Science cannot operate in isolation and must always be seen within the social, ethical, cultural and religious views of the time.

Consider having a class split into a 'jury', 'Galileo and his sympathizers' and 'the church'. When you have researched the arguments and the science, the class could 'act out' Galileo's trial. This could form part of a cross-curricular session drawing on history, PHSE, citizenship and religious studies.

Engaging activities

It is often difficult to develop practical activities for some areas of science in school. While most pupils are interested in space, the lack of practical activity can be off-putting. The following two activities can be used to re-engage the students.

Model solar system

A great activity for a dry day is to asssign the students a planet. Because there are only eight to go around, some with have to share. Then, with you being the Sun, take the class on to a sports field and have them space themselves out using a scale to reflect the planets' distances from the Sun. Table 11.3 could be your starting point. However, you and your students will be able, no doubt, to devise a better one!

Constellations

A good revision exercise for work on electricity (especially simple circuits) is to have the students build a model constellation.

Choose a constellation. Draw out the brightest stars, in their relative positions, on A3 black card. Use a cork borer or similar to make holes where the stars are to be set out. Make these holes large enough to take a small bulb. Design and build a circuit to light the number of bulbs being used as stars. Fix the bulbs in place and view from the back of a darkened room. Can the other students identify the constellation?

Table 11.3   *Sun–planet distances*

Planet	Sun–planet distance (millions of km)	Suitable scale (m)
Mercury	57	2
Venus	107	4
Earth	150	5
Mars	229	8
Jupiter	777	27
Saturn	1430	50
Uranus	2870	100
Neptune	4500	156

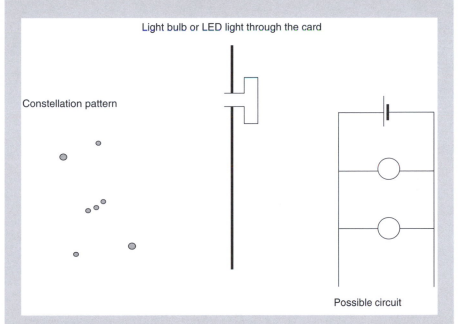

Figure 11.5   Modelling constellations

As an extension to this activity, the students could be asked to control the brightness of the 'stars' in their constellation to match that observed in the night sky. To do this, you could use bulbs of different power ratings; put resistors in series with the bulbs; or remodel the constellation using white LED (light-emitting diode) light (see Figure 11.5).

Further reading

Morison, I. (2008) *Introduction to Astronomy and Cosmology.* Oxford: Wiley.

12 Global warming?
Gren Ireson

This chapter covers:

- the Earth's atmosphere
- global warming
- changes in sea level
- the ozone layer
- CFCS and greeenhouse gases.

 Test your own knowledge

Before reading the material in this chapter test your current knowledge with the following questions:

1. What is a greenhouse gas?
2. What impact is global warming likely to have on a) polar ice caps; b) sea level?
3. How did the Earth's atmosphere come about in the first place?
4. What is ozone and why is it important?
5. Some people argue that changes in the 'ozone layer' are reseponsible for increased numbers of skin cancers. What else could explain this rise?

Atmosphere basics

The atmosphere on the Earth is thought to have evolved from the time when the Earth was cool enough to allow one to form. Early in its evolution the Earth was very hot. In fact, it was molten, and any gas molecules had so

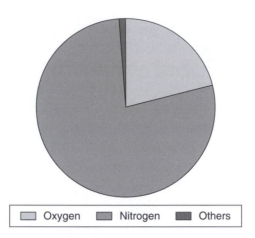

Oxygen   Nitrogen   Others

Figure 12.1 Composition of the Earth's atmosphere

much kinetic energy that they could escape the gravitational force of the planet and simply *fly off* into space.

When the Earth cooled to form a solid crust, some gas molecules could be captured. These gases came from what we would now call volcanoes and consisted mainly of water vapour (H_2O), carbon dioxide (CO_2), ammonia and nitrogen molecules (N_2).

It is believed that light from the Sun broke down the ammonia, releasing more nitrogen into the atmosphere over a period of several billion years. Early bacteria on Earth – *Cyanobacteria* – photosynthesized under sunlight, extracting CO_2 and releasing O_2 into the atmosphere leading to the 21% oxygen and 78% nitrogen seen today (see Figure 12.1).

Global warming

There is currently no definitive answer to the question of global warming. Some scientists argue that the global temperature is cyclical, while others argue that the global mean is increasing faster than past trends. Figure 12.2 shows the five-year average temperature, based on instrument records, for the Northern Atmosphere, while Figure 12.3 shows the estimated global mean from 1000 to 2000, again for the Northern Hemisphere we didn't have instruments before about 1850.

Sea-level change

Sea level has always varied over time and, again, some argue that this is evidence of the cycle of global temperature change, although seismic

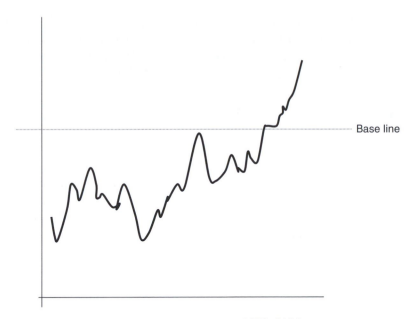

Figure 12.2   Five-year average temperature, 1850–2000

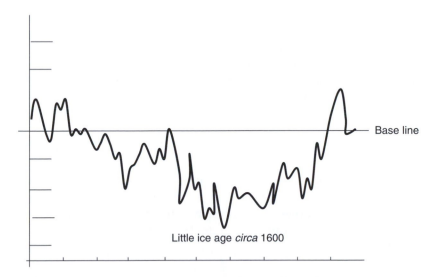

Figure 12.3   Mean global temperature, Northern Hemisphere, 1000–2000

changes can bring about sea-level change. Isostatic changes – that is, changes due to the subsidence or uplift of landmass – can have an effect on sea level. In the UK, Scotland is still recovering from the last ice age:

as the ice retreats the mass decreases, and Scotland is rising at about 1 mm per year. Southeast England, however, is 'sinking' at the same rate. Eustatic changes – that is, changes due to either polarice melting or seafloor spreading – also have an effect on the global sea level.

The ozone layer and CFC's?

When sunlight is incident on the Earth, the Earth's surface becomes warmer. This heat energy is redistributed by the action of wind and ocean currents. How much energy is reflected back into space is called albedo, and this varies greatly (see Table 12.1).

Table 12.1   *Albedo*

Surface	Albedo (% reflected)
Snow	~90
Ice	~30
Desert	~40
Forests	~17
Water	~5

However all this is a tight balancing act between absorbed and reflected energy, where ozone (O_3) protects the Earth from harmful radiation from the Sun. Other gases, especially CO_2 and methane (CH_4), can trap too much energy, leading to a 'runaway' effect on global temperature.

Ozone absorbs ultra violet radiation (UV) and breaks down into an oxygen molecule and an oxygen atom. These then recombine to form ozone:

$$\text{UV radiation} \quad \left\{ \begin{array}{l} O_3 \rightarrow O_2 + O \\ O_3 \rightarrow O + O_2 \end{array} \right\} O_3$$

This is fine while the balance of ozone in the atmosphere is maintained. Unfortunately some chemical products (for example, chlorofluorocarbons or CFCs) break down the ozone in the atmosphere more quickly than it recombines, leading to a reduction in the ozone available to protect the Earth.

CFCs and free radicals

One common CFC – called dichlorodifluoromethane or CCl_2F_2 – was widely used as both a refrigerant and a propellant in aerosols of all kinds since it is unreactive and non-toxic. Unfortunately once it gets into the atmosphere it is broken down, just like the ozone, but in such a way as to form 'free radicals'. You may recall from Section 2 that some molecules form covalent bonds where they 'share' electrons. Hydrogen is usually found in this state with two atoms, each with one electron, forming the stable and neutral H_2 molecule. If the H_2 is broken down we could get a negative ion, H^-, with both the electrons, and a positive ion, H^+, with no electrons. If, however, the H_2 molecule breaks down so as to give one electron to each of the pair of ions, it creates a very, very reactive substance. An unpaired outer electron also makes for high reactivity. Chemists called this a free radical and show it as $H\cdot$ or H dot.

When ultra violet radiation acts on the CCl_2F_2 molecule it produces not hydrogen but chlorine and free radicals, Cl, as follows:

$$Cl\cdot + O_3 \rightarrow ClO + O_2$$
$$ClO + O_3 \rightarrow 2O_2 + Cl\cdot$$

Notice how the chlorine-free radical is recycled. This is an additional part of the problem: the impact of the CFC lasts for a long, long, time.

How science works

We have seen that ozone is important in the atmosphere to protect the Earth from UV radiation and that CFCs and other pollutants can reduce the amount of ozone in the atmosphere. However, at ground level, ozone can be a problem, causing irritation both to people's skin and to their respiratory tracts. Unfortunately both photocopiers and laser printers produce ozone.

The students could be asked to research the effect of ozone on people prior to role playing either a laser printer salesperson or a health and safety officer.

CO_2 now and then

The study of artic ice cores suggests that, prior to the Industrial Revolution, the atmosphere contained 280 parts per million (ppm) CO_2, but now this figure is 387 ppm. While this may seem a small change the rate of change is increasing, and it is the impact CO_2 and other 'greenhouse gases' has on the atmosphere that is important.

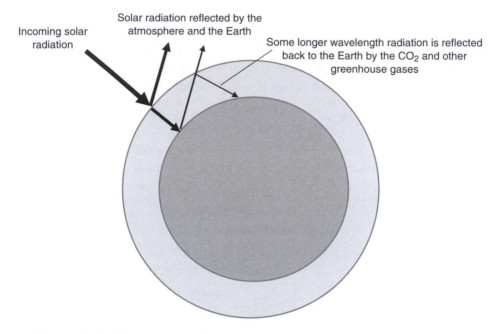

Figure 12.4   The trapping of heat by greenhouse gases

Solar radiation from the Sun is incident on the Earth and its atmosphere, with some being reflected by the atmosphere and some by the Earth's surface (see Figure 12.4). However, some solar radiation is absorbed by the Earth and reradiated as longer wavelength infrared radiation. It is this longer wavelength radiation that is 'trapped' by the green house gases (such as carbon dioxide) which is believed to be a cause of climate change by global warming.

Engaging activity

The effect of CO_2 on temperature change can easily be shown by placing a temperature probe (under a few centimetres of sand) into each of two conical flasks. Place both flasks under a 100 W desk lamp and observe the temperature change. Now introduce CO_2 into one of the flasks and continue to observe.

Further reading

Armstrong, D., Mugglestone, F., Richards, R. and Stratton, F. (2008) *OCR Geology*. Harlow: Pearson Education.
An excellent summary of the geological knowledge required at A-level and a good starting point for those wanting to improve their geological knowledge including issues of global warming.

Index

Exciting Early Years and Primary Texts from SAGE

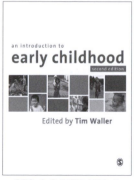

978-1-84787-518-1

978-1-84787-393-4

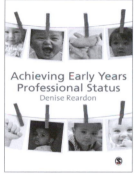

978-1-84787-190-9

978-1-84787-524-2

978-1-84860-127-7

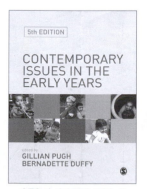

978-1-84787-593-8

978-1-84860-119-2

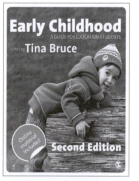

978-1-84860-224-3

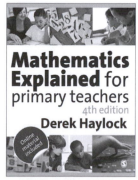

978-1-84860-197-0

Find out more about these titles and our wide range of books for education students and practitioners at **www.sagepub.co.uk/education**

Exciting Education Texts from SAGE

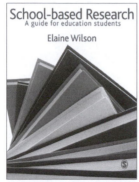

978-1-4129-4850-0

978-1-4129-4818-0

978-1-84787-917-2

978-1-84787-018-6

978-1-84787-943-1

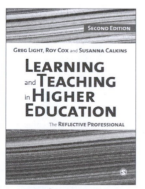

978-1-84860-008-9

978-1-84787-362-0

978-1-84787-289-0

978-1-84920-076-9

Find out more about these titles and our wide range of books for education students and practitioners at **www.sagepub.co.uk/education**